HOW TO
GIVE YOUR
CHILD A GREAT
SELF-IMAGE

HOW TO GIVE YOUR CHILD A GREAT SELF-IMAGE

DR. DEBORA PHILLIPS
WITH FRED A. BERNSTEIN

RANDOM HOUSE
NEW YORK

Library of Congress Cataloging-in-Publication Data

Phillips, Debora.
How to give your child a great self-image / by Debora Phillips
with Fred A. Bernstein.
p. cm.
ISBN 0-394-57478-8
1. Behavior therapy for children.   2. Self-respect in children.
I. Bernstein, Fred A.   II. Title.
RJ505.B4P57   1989
155.4' 1825—dc20   88-43220
CIP

Manufactured in the United States of America
9 8 7 6 5 4 3 2
First Edition

To MB,
who would have had a
better life if she had loved
herself as much as everyone
around her loved her.

PREFACE

How to Give Your Child a Great Self-Image is based on the principles of behavior therapy. Behavior therapy, a modern psycho-
therapy grounded in scientific knowledge about learning,
proceeds from the basic assumption that nearly all human behavior is learned. Relearning, through methods developed by
behavior therapists, can enable people to change behavior that
causes them pain.

Using behavior therapy, a wide range of emotional problems
can be cured—not merely controlled, or coped with, or understood, but fundamentally removed. This approach works as well
for children as it does for adults.

Behavior therapy uses experimentally established principles
of learning to change unadaptive behavior (in children, such
behavior might include the inability to make friends, or an ob-

session with grades) and unadaptive feelings (fear of rejection, general hopelessness, or extreme sensitivity to teasing). Behavior therapy can weaken behavior that causes children anxiety or hinders their ability to function comfortably in their environment and can strengthen behavior that helps them pursue their lives more happily and more completely.

Because emotional behavior is learned at a primitive (subcortical) level of neural organization, change must take place at this same primitive level. No matter how clearly you may see that a particular behavior is unhelpful to your child—and no matter how logically you explain that to your child—he may not be capable of behaving in a different fashion. Emotional habits are resistant to logical arguments or good advice, because something that is learned emotionally cannot be unlearned on a purely intellectual level.

This book applies the techniques of behavior therapy to a particular set of human responses: feelings of inadequacy or low self-worth. Children who tend to dwell on their own shortcomings will learn behaviors that will free them from that destructive pattern. Those who have difficulty socially, or who are unable to perform up to their potential, will learn methods for overcoming those problems.

However, this is not a book about how professionals can help your child. This book will show *you* how to give your child the help he needs. In doing so, it will dramatically improve the quality of communication between you and your child.

How to Give Your Child a Great Self-Image has all the virtues of behavior therapy: brevity, action, and a systematic, step-by-step program to reach specific goals. It demonstrates one of the great strengths of behavior therapy—dealing with large, complex emotional difficulties in manageable component parts. Moreover, its clarity, warmth, and understanding make the techniques of behavior therapy both accessible and useful to any concerned parent.

—Joseph Wolpe, M.D.
Professor of Psychiatry
Medical College of Pennsylvania
Philadelphia

ACKNOWLEDGMENTS

How to Give Your Child a Great Self-Image is the product of many people's efforts.

The children and parents I have counseled over the years are the true source of much of the material in this book. By letting me into their lives, they showed me how much a self-image improvement program could accomplish. Though I have changed their names to protect their privacy, I have not forgotten all the wonderful things they have taught me.

Dr. Joseph Wolpe, the father of behavior therapy, developed the theories and principles that guide this work. *How to Give Your Child a Great Self-Image* is the direct outgrowth of his pioneering research, which has informed and inspired me throughout my working life.

Many other professionals helped build the foundation on which my work in behavior therapy rests. In particular, the ideas of Dr. B. F. Skinner are seen in the chapter on positive reinforcement. The hand of Dr. Joseph Cautela can be felt in the use of positive imagery in many parts of this book, and Dr. Wesley Becker's classroom studies in the early seventies inspired me to think about the need for further research on self-image, from which this book eventually resulted.

Other friends and colleagues made valuable contributions:

Fred Bernstein did more than simply write down my ideas. He inspired me and challenged me and made this truly a collaborative effort.

Andrew Lang, a skilled editor and a wonderful friend, lent his expertise to this manuscript even when he really didn't have the time.

Carol Thompson applied her intelligence, perceptions and insights to the manuscript, making this a more usable book.

Richard Brown lent his enthusiastic support.

Merle Feld, one of the world's great people, added immediacy, compassion and realism to this book; her ideas are reflected on every page.

Stella Wolpe, a gracious and loving woman—and a first-rate editor—was generous with her time and talents.

Robert Judd, my collaborator on two previous books, taught me that I could popularize my work without compromising it.

Becky Saletan, my editor at Random House, demonstrated her thoughtfulness and intelligence from the very first discussion of this project until its completion. She is a rare editor who takes the time to go over a manuscript sentence by sentence, improving it in countless ways.

I would like to give special thanks to four people whose understanding and support made it possible for me to write this book:

My brother, Michael, for accepting and loving me unconditionally, which contributed so much to my own self-image.

My children, Ron and Wendy, for demonstrating the importance of a great self-image in their beauty as human beings.

Dennis J. Munjack, for fine-tuning the manuscript and for much, much more.

—Dr. Deborah Phillips
Princeton, N.J.

CONTENTS

HOW TO
GIVE YOUR
CHILD A GREAT
SELF-IMAGE

INTRODUCTION

In seventeen years of professional practice, I have worked with hundreds of children, from infancy through adolescence. I have counseled straight-A students, talented musicians, and world-class athletes. And I have rarely met one who couldn't benefit from an improved self-image.

What do you want your child to be?

There may be days when you want her to be

tall
rich
an astronaut
a star
a gourmet chef

a doctor

a lawyer

a millionaire.

But what you really want your child to be is happy.

The happiest people you know don't necessarily have the best jobs, or the most money, or even the best health. Their "secret," as you may already know, is self-esteem. They feel lovable, valuable, worthy. They have the strength to deal with life's inevitable setbacks. They're happy because they're happy with themselves.

That's why you want your child to have a great self-image.

If you're a parent with a great self-image, you have most likely enjoyed professional success, satisfying relationships, and the knowledge that you can get many of the things you want out of life. Feeling good about yourself enables you to treat yourself, and those around you, kindly.

Now that you're a parent, you want your child to have as good a self-image as you do.

If you are a parent with a less-than-great self-image, you may think of yourself as a failure in your personal or professional life (regardless of how successful you are). You struggle against self-doubt and feelings of inadequacy. You are hard on yourself, and you may be hard on others. Every day is spent fighting the feeling that you're unworthy.

You want your child to grow up with a better self-image than you have.

If you're like most parents, there's nothing you wouldn't do to give your child a great self-image. But . . .

You don't know how.

Until now, no one's shown you how to improve your child's self-image. You may have studied music, or art, or accounting, but chances are you have never taken a course in parenting (and you've certainly never taken one in how to give your child a better self-image).

So how can you translate your good intentions into actions?

This book will show you how. Lots of books talk about the importance of giving your child a great self-image. But they never tell you how to go about it. This book picks up where the others leave off. It contains the first step-by-step program for improving your child's self-image. This book will help you become the kind of parent you always said you'd be. It is easy to read and easy to use, and best of all, it works. It is based on techniques I have been developing since 1972. I have used them on hundreds of children, and I know that you can use them, too.

You don't need years of training to use the principles of behavior therapy to help your child. You don't need an office, a couch, or a certificate on the wall. The techniques in the book are straightforward enough for anyone to use. If you want to help your child, you're qualified to do so (in fact, *no one* is more qualified than you).

You don't have time.

You and your children probably have too many things to do already.

The office keeps you late night after night.
Your daughter has basketball practice after school.
The phone rings and your son (whom you had hoped to talk to) is tied up in heavy intrigue for an hour.
The car's not running right.
Wet laundry lies at the bottom of the washing machine like a sullen accusation.

This book will help you make time. Putting this book to work will take just ten minutes a day. That's probably less time then you're spending now

- worrying about your child's problems
- talking about your child's problems
- trying to get your child to change—and not succeeding
- locked in unproductive communication
- fretting about your shortcomings as a parent

You're frightened.

It's scary to watch your child grow up with a less-than-great self-image. You're afraid he won't be happy or successful, that he won't ever feel good about himself.

This book will help you replace that normal parental fear with a specific plan of action. Starting today, you will learn

1. to teach your child to feel better about himself as a person.
2. to improve your child's view of her abilities, intelligence, and appearance.
3. to enable your child to accept compliments without discounting them and to deal with criticism, teasing, or rejection without feeling defeated or defensive.
4. to improve communication and goodwill between you and your child.
5. to help yourself feel better, more competent, more in control as a parent.
6. to begin to solve your child's most stubborn problems.

If your child

- is sometimes uncommunicative
- has trouble making friends

- doesn't live up to his potential
- is aggressive
- often seems angry
- is shy
- seems scared of many things

improving his self-image may be the fastest way to help him.

You may be amazed by how powerful the techniques in this book can be.

Parents of children I've worked with have told me:

"You weren't working on his grades, but suddenly they're better."

"You weren't trying to change her social skills, but suddenly she has more friends."

"You were working with my son. But suddenly communication in our family is so much better that my relationship with my daughter is improving.

Why a great self-image?

A great self-image is the single most important tool for successfully facing the problems, issues, and crises that arise in everyday life. Self-image is central to how your child learns, achieves, works, socializes, and loves. Self-image is the key to the way your child treats himself and is treated by others.

Self-image determines

- How your child does in school. In one important study of elementary-school children, self-image proved to be a better predictor of grades than did IQ.
- What your child chooses to do with his life. To a child with a low self-image, many options seem closed.
- How and what your child achieves. A child who believes she can, can.

- Whom your child loves, and how well.
- How your child socializes and whom she chooses as friends.
- How your child deals with peer pressure. *There has been a lot of talk about saying no to drugs. But almost no one has talked about what makes some children capable of saying no. The answer is a strong self-image.*

Can a good self-image really be taught?

Anything that is learned can be unlearned, changed, improved, relearned. *That is the underlying principle of behavior therapy—and of this book.*

And your child's self-image *is* learned. Every time your child is

+		−
praised	or	criticized
welcomed	or	rejected
accepted	or	teased
loved	or	hated
listened to	or	ignored

his self-image is

made better   or   made worse.

Unfortunately, in many children's lives, the minuses outweigh the pluses.

The minuses

Your child is teased, criticized, or rejected far more often than you'd like . . .

By his teachers: According to one study, almost 90 percent of what teachers say to children in the classroom is negative.

By her playmates: Teasing is a cruel reality for many children, particularly the ones whose self-images are already at risk. If your child is too tall, too short, too smart, the "wrong" color or religion, he may be a victim of teasing.

By society at large: In the media, all complexions are clear, all stomachs are flat. Children are made to feel inadequate by constant exposure to images of perfection.

By you: No matter how hard you try, you can't avoid sending your child messages that damage her self-image. You reject her (simply leaving her with a babysitter is rejection). You ignore her (you can't possibly listen to everything she says—or always give her the reaction she wants). And you criticize her, no matter how hard you try not to . . .

It's natural for you to criticize your child. It's natural to berate your child for a messy room or untied shoes, or to tell him that he's not as smart, or as coordinated, or as polite, as you'd like him to be. You criticize your child to change his behavior, or just to let him know you're angry. It certainly isn't your intention to hurt his self-image, but that may be what you're doing.

The pluses

This book will teach you to provide the pluses in your child's life—the praise, the empathy, the encouragement that will give him a better self-image. *If you feel that you're part of the problem, this book will help you become part of the solution.*

Who this book is for

1. *Every child who can use a great self-image:* In my experience, that's *every* child. So don't be embarrassed that your child needs this help. Feel good about the fact that you were wise enough to recognize the opportunity for change.

2. *Children at any stage of development, from birth through adolescence:* It's never too early to begin using this book. Your child's

self-esteem began developing the moment he was born—and by applying the techniques in this book soon enough, you can make sure it develops beautifully the first time.

If your child already shows signs of a poor self-image, you may need to correct old behaviors, to reteach rather than simply teach. This book will show you how to do that, too.

3. *"Normal" children:* This isn't a book about solving the problems of disturbed children. It's about making sure "normal" children develop as wonderfully as they can. Of course, "normal" covers a lot of ground, and many normal children have problems. I have often found that with children who are aggressive, uncooperative, or lethargic, an improved self-image can have a lasting and dramatic impact.

There is no child who can't be helped by the techniques in this book. However, if you feel your child is deeply troubled, he may also need professional help.

BEHAVIOR THERAPY: SOME KEY CONCEPTS

As a behavior therapist, I am skilled in helping people change feelings and behaviors that are causing them discomfort. And I have developed an arsenal of techniques with which to do that.

It will help if you understand a few principles of behavior therapy before you begin to use this book.

The feeling follows the doing

If you've ever told a friend who's feeling down, "Instead of just lying around, get out of bed, put some nice clothes on, and go out and do something fun," you understand one of the principles of behavior therapy: By changing people's actions, you can change their feelings.

This book asks you to teach your child some of the behaviors associated with a good self-image. As your child learns those behaviors, feelings of improved self-worth will follow. For example, you may want your child to feel calm and secure in the face of teasing. The first step in that process is to teach him to act calm and secure; once he does, he'll begin to *feel* as confident as he seems.

Positive reinforcement

Whenever you praise someone for doing something, you are giving him an incentive to do it again. Throughout this book, you will be asked to praise your child for trying behaviors that lead to a better self-image. For instance, you may want your child to learn to accept a compliment correctly. You'll tell him what you'd like him to do, then have him try it. If he does what you asked him to do, you'll praise him ("That's terrific." "Great." "I'm so proud.") Your praise will make him want to keep accepting compliments correctly.

To encourage people to learn important skills, it sometimes helps to give them tangible rewards. Throughout this book, I suggest rewarding your child for learning new, better behaviors. These rewards don't have to be big. You can use pennies, nickels, or dimes. Or you can use points—with twenty points adding up to a trip to the zoo, or a new model airplane. For example, if you want your child to write down things she likes about herself (in order to get her to focus on her strengths), you may offer her a point for every strength she writes down. Are you bribing your child? Not at all. You're just rewarding her for helping you give her a new self-image.

Repetition

Most learning takes place through repetition. The best way to make a new skill or feeling second nature is to practice it over and over again. That's why, throughout this book, I will ask you to repeat certain exercises and certain steps of the techniques, some of them dozens of times. For instance, you may want your child to learn to say good things about himself. But he may feel uncomfortable talking about himself in a favorable light. To lessen that discomfort, you may have to ask him The Question ("Tell me something you like about yourself"; chapter 2), four times a day for a week.

Modeling

One of the best ways to learn a new behavior is to watch somebody else (particularly someone you admire) demonstrate that behavior. That's why, throughout the book, I will ask you to "model" the behaviors you want your child to learn. For instance, you may want your child to be able to speak kindly of her appearance—not to be so hard on her looks. One of the most effective ways to do that is for you to model the correct behavior. ("Well, I'm no movie star, but I'm pretty happy with the way I look.") Your child will learn from your example.

Behavior rehearsal

Knowing what to do in uncomfortable situations can make a person feel competent and in control. Before "sending" your child out into the world to grapple with such self-image killers as criticism and teasing, you will help her rehearse the behaviors you'd like her to use. For instance, you may want to show her how to "stand tall" in the face of persistent criticism from a teacher. One good way to do that is to rehearse the scene at home ("Okay, I'll play your teacher, and let's see how you react when I criticize you.") before she tries it in the classroom.

Hierarchy

You don't teach someone to ski by pushing him off the top of the mountain. He'll learn more easily (and comfortably) if you start him on a "bunny slope," then gradually work your way up to steeper runs. Throughout the book, you'll be asked to tackle your child's problems in the same way: first, rank situations from least to most painful; then work on them in that order. For instance, some rejections may hurt your child a little, some a lot, and some so much that they require immediate intervention. By ranking the rejections on a hierarchy, you'll know the best order in which to tackle them.

Numbers

There are times when I'll ask you to do something a specific number of times.

"Give your child *four* compliments a day." (Not three, not five).

"Have your child write down *ten* things she likes about herself."

There's a reason for the numbers. I have found, in years of practice, that if I say, "Compliment your child more often," most parents won't do it. They may *want* to do it, but the advice seems too vague, or the task too enormous. But if I say, "Compliment your child *four* times a day," most parents will do it, because I've given them a specific, manageable task. So it's not that four compliments are so much better than three or five. The reason I give numbers is to make it easier for you to begin using the techniques.

A final note:

You have the hardest job in the world. If you've toilet trained a child, or held his hand after a nightmare, or waited for her to come home from her first date—you know how difficult your job can be. You also know that the rewards of being a parent are elusive. You can't count on your child thanking you, much less paying you back. The only thing that makes your job do-able is the satisfaction you get from seeing your child become competent, successful, happy. You'll get more of that satisfaction than you imagined if you give your child a great self-image.

‧‧

HOW TO USE
THIS BOOK

How to Give Your Child a Great Self-Image is a book about avoiding problems, about helping your child develop beautifully right from the start. But it is also a book about *solving* problems: if your child is a victim of teasing, or is unhappy with his appearance, or feels sensitive to rejection, this book will show you how to give him immediate and specific help.

Some of the problems children face are age-related. (For instance, poor body image is frequently a problem of adolescence.) But children's temperaments and experiences vary so greatly that there is no easy way to predict when or why a problem may arise. (If you have more than one child, you know how different two human beings can be.) One child may be a victim of teasing at five; another at fifteen. One seven-year-old may stand up to strong criticism without wavering, while another wilts at the slightest sign of disapproval. The techniques in this book can be used with children of any age. The case histories I've included are meant to show how *some* parents have helped *some* children, but that's all. You can easily adapt the techniques to the age of your child. (You may need to adjust your vocabulary, but little else. The principles are universal.)

If your child is four or under: You have the luxury of time. Start by reading chapter 1, which contains specific advice for working with infants and toddlers. Then continue on through the rest of the book. It may be too early to use some of the techniques, particularly in the later chapters, but reading them will prepare you to deal with situations as they arise in your family. You'll have the advantage of knowing what to do before you have to do it.

If your child is five or six: He's old enough to benefit from virtually all the techniques in this book. If you're not facing a serious crisis that requires you to skip ahead, start by reading (and working on) chapters 2, 3, and 4, which will teach you the "building block skills" that come up again and again in the rest of the book. Then continue reading—and teaching your child— at your own pace.

If your child is seven or older: She may be exhibiting specific behaviors that require immediate attention. Read chapters 2, 3, and 4, which will "prep" you for the rest of the book. Then skip ahead focusing on the chapters and techniques that will enable you to have the most immediate effect on your child's behavior. Later, when you have time, return to the chapters you skipped.

If you have more than one child: You can use this book with two or more children at the same time. But since each child (and each parent-child relationship) is different, you may want to work with them individually at first, setting aside, say, ten minutes a day to "meet" privately with each child. Your six-year-old may need help answering The Question (chapter 2), while your ten-year-old may need to learn to accept compliments better (chapter 5), and your twelve-year-old needs to work on improving her body image as she enters adolescence (chapter 9). However, once all of your children are on the road to a better self-image and can express their feelings comfortably, begin holding weekly round-table discussions at which they can talk about their problems. The round table (with the help of a few peacekeeping rules) will breed sibling cooperation (instead of sibling rivalry) and will enable you to help all your children at once.

Work at your own pace.

You may be able to get through each chapter in about a month. (That means you'll need about a year to "finish" all eleven chapters.) When I wrote this book, that's the pace I had in mind.

But a-chapter-a-month is only a suggestion. You should work at whatever pace is most comfortable for you. No one's watching you or grading you. The only thing that matters is whether your child's self-image is improving.

Here are a few "instructions" to keep in mind as you begin using this book:

Make mistakes.

The techniques in this book are as new to you as they are to your child. Don't expect to be able to handle them perfectly the first time. If you make mistakes, your child will still love you. (Indeed, all of chapter 10 is about the importance of letting your child know you aren't perfect.) No one's testing you. This book wasn't written for the mythical "perfect parent." It was written for you, a real parent who's trying to do the best she can in an imperfect world.

Get help.

Many of the techniques are easier to teach if there's another adult giving you help and reinforcement. If you're married, try to enlist your spouse. (Even if he doesn't have time to read the book, he can help you with specific projects. For example, he can learn to compliment your child four times a day regardless of whether he's read the chapter on positive reinforcement.) If you're a single parent, you'll have more work to do. (So what else is new?) If you can, get a friend or relative to help you.

It's also a great idea to try to involve your child's teachers and others who have a role in shaping his self-image in your program to boost it. If you think, for example, that your child's teacher is overly critical in the classroom, empathize with her ("I know how hard your job is.") and give her positive reinforcement ("It's really nice of you to talk to me about Steven's self-image."). Then ask her to help you implement the techniques in this book.

The benefits to your child will be multiplied if he sees that two (or even three adults) care enough about his development to work with him on his self-image.

How do you know if your child needs professional help? There's no easy answer to that question, which is why it's important to be cautious. If your child seems extremely depressed or anxious, or if those feelings last for more than a couple of days, or if they interfere with his normal functioning—seek help.

Don't hide this book.

There's nothing wrong with what you're doing; you don't have to keep it a secret from your child (or anyone else). In fact, you can tell your child as much about this book as he's able to understand. And if he wants to read some of it, why not let him?

Note: Since you don't have to hide this book, you won't need to know the techniques by heart in order to teach them to your child. Feel free to refer to the book as often as you need to. Your goal is to help your child—not to impress him with your powers of memorization.

Don't be intimidated.

As you read this book, you may encounter a few "perfect" parents—parents who praise but never criticize, who never become angry, who listen patiently day after day.

The parents in this book are meant to be "models" for you in exactly the same way I want you to "model" healthy behavior for your child. They are meant to inspire, not intimidate you. Don't worry if you can't be just like them. Aspire to do better, sure, but don't feel you have to be superhuman.

Keep at it.

Some of the techniques in this book may feel awkward at first. Many new skills are like that. For instance, you may feel odd praising your child about little things (just as you felt odd the first time you typed or skied or rode a bike). Don't abandon a technique because it doesn't seem natural—or doesn't seem to be working—the first time you try it. Give each new technique a chance—a few days or, better yet, a few weeks—to begin to have the desired impact on your child.

Respect your child's privacy.

As you work your way through this book, you will find yourself asking your child about his thoughts and feelings. In order to help him, you need to know what's on his mind.

There may be some subjects he doesn't want to talk about, however. If he wants to change the subject, let him. Encourage him to open up—but don't push him. You'll accomplish a lot more, in the long run, if your child feels completely comfortable with what you're doing.

Accept your child's uniqueness.

Don't feel guilty if you find you can't use all these techniques with your child, or if you don't get the exact results you hoped for. You can't control everything your child does or becomes. You child's natural temperament has a lot to do with how well he responds to your efforts. Still, no matter what your child's temperament, you can have a tremendous impact on his development using the techniques in this book to bolster his self-image.

Tolerate your child's mistakes.

I don't expect you to teach every technique in this book perfectly, and you can't expect your child to learn them perfectly, either. Your child doesn't have to do everything (or anything) right the first time. Let him make mistakes. Let him know he's human. Dwell on his successes, not his failures.

Innovate.

The techniques in this book are the ones I have used with the most success. However, they aren't the only way to improve your child's self-image. If you come up with new techniques, I'd love to know about them. Feel free to write to me, Dr. Debora Phillips, at 211 North Harrison Street, Princeton, New Jersey 08540, or 435 North Bedford Drive, Suite 403, Beverly Hills, California 90210.

Have fun.

Don't take anything I say so seriously that you forget to have fun with your child. Enjoying your relationship with your child is what this book is all about.

Don't forget yourself.

If your own self-image isn't great, you know how painful that can be.

Your immediate goal is to help your child. But as you do so, you'll find your own self-image becoming stronger. Once you see how much difference you can make in your child's life, you'll feel wonderfully confident as a parent. When you give your child a great self-image, there's no end to the good things that can happen for *you*.

1

A STRONG FOUNDATION

At an outdoor market in Seattle, I watched an old man sell a wooden puzzle to a woman in her twenties.

"Who's it for?" asked the man, as he searched for a bag.

"For my son," the woman said. "He's two."

"Are you going to help him with it?" the old man continued.

"I guess so," said the woman. "Shouldn't I?"

"Absolutely not," replied the man. "It's essential that you let him work it out alone. Don't help him. Don't put in any of the pieces for him, and don't tell him what to do. Be patient."

"Why can't I help him?" asked the woman.

"Because it's not the puzzle that's important," said the man. "What is important is your son's self-image."

"Self-image?" asked the woman.

"Sure," said the old man. "I see many new parents. They're always in a hurry. They don't give their children the time to learn things for themselves. If you do that, your son will never have a chance to develop a good self-image."

"I suppose you're right," said the woman. "It won't be easy, but I'll try to let him finish the puzzle himself."

"Good," said the man. "Don't worry about how long it takes him, as long as he feels good about what he's doing. Unless he asks for help, don't give it to him. And tell him how glad you are to see him trying."

"Okay," said the woman. "I'll do that."

As I walked away, I marveled at the old man's wisdom.

He had given the woman a blueprint for nurturing a good self-image in her child.

Like that Seattle mother, you may not have realized that a positive self-image is best taught long before your child learns to read, or write, or ride a bike.

In fact, it's never too early to start working on your child's self-image. By eighteen months, your child will have a strong sense of himself and his place in the family. And by the time he's three, his self-image may determine his ability to make new friends, to play with others, and to learn new things.

You're the teacher.

You have a lot of things to teach your child in the next few years: how to talk, how to crawl, how to use a fork and spoon, how to read, how to tie a shoelace, how to play baseball . . .

Is how to have a great self-image on your list?

While all the other things can wait, teaching your child how to have a great self-image can't.

Start by praising your child at least four times a day.

Nothing will do more for your child's self-esteem than a regular diet of praise (positive reinforcement).

Read the rules for giving praise on pages 38–43, and follow as many of them as you can.

Praise him for trying.
Praise her for improving.
Praise him just for being him.
Praise her when she least expects it.

Your child is never too young to benefit from praise.

Long before your child can understand your words (words like "wonderful" and "terrific") he'll know, from your attitude, your posture, and your tone of voice, that you're telling him that you think he's wonderful and terrific. And that knowledge will begin to build up his self-image.

When you don't want to use words, you can praise your child by

- holding her securely
- smiling at him warmly
- giving her small rewards
- rocking him
- cuddling her
- singing to him
- speaking in a "praiseful" tone of voice.

What's there to praise? She's still in diapers.

Okay, so she can't bring home straight A's, or score a touchdown, or play a sonata. But there is no end to the list of things you will find to praise if you look at:

How regularly she sleeps

How carefully he observes the world

How adorably she gurgles

How many steps he takes

How long she stands

How persistently he works at learning

How passionately she responds to music

How warmly he responds to your touch.

Don't wait for him to run the four-minute mile or write a poem. (If you do, you'll have waited too long.)

Actively seek out things to praise.

Praise the effort. Compliment your child for trying, for making progress, for learning new things.

Hug him because he stood up for ten seconds (even though you'd like it to be twenty).

Cuddle her for sleeping halfway through the night (even though you wanted it to be the whole night).

Smile at him for learning a new word (even if it's the only word he's learned this week).

Compliment her for working so hard on the puzzle (even if you know she didn't solve it).

Let your child learn at her own pace.

Don't worry about how fast your child is learning to talk or walk or play with dolls.

Barring any serious developmental problems, as long as your child is being stimulated by the things and the people around him, he's learning enough; specific educational achievements can come later.

At three, Zachary said "aminal" instead of "animal." His mother didn't correct him. (She figured he'd have lots of time to learn the right pronunciation.) She wanted him to "grow" a good self-image, and that meant, at least for now, avoiding the word *wrong*.

When Jane, two, hammered a peg into the wrong hole, her father didn't say, "You did that wrong. Let me show you." Instead he said, "You tried so nicely to do that, and you had so much fun doing it. I'm really proud."

When Mark, four, started reciting the alphabet with "A, B, G, D, E," his mother didn't correct him. She knew he would learn to say the alphabet correctly soon enough, and she wanted him to feel that he had learned it on his own.

Some parents I know would have said, "No, it's A, B, *C*, D, E." If you're one of them, I know you're well-intentioned. You want your child to learn as much as possible, as quickly as possible. But if you slow down a little, give your child a chance to find his own way through the alphabet—you might find that he's learned something a lot more valuable than "A, B, C, D, E."

So if you can, stop using the word *wrong*. Replace it with the phrase "good try," and see how beautifully your child's self-image develops.

Leave criticism out of it.

You have the hardest job in the world. You're exhausted or exasperated more than you'd like to admit. Just getting your child to bed at night can be a struggle. With a toddler, there's a lot to criticize, a lot to complain about, a lot to make you weary. Still, focusing on the negative ("This is a disaster." "I can't stand this anymore." "Are you going to pull this every night?")

is not the answer. It certainly doesn't help anyone's self-image (since you want to be a fair, competent parent, *your* self-image is as much on the line as your child's).

Here are some ways to focus on the positive:

"I know you can get into bed now, and if you do, I'll read you a story."

(*Not* "Why are you taking so long to go to sleep?")

"If you help me give you a bath, I'll let you watch ten minutes of *Sesame Street*. Why don't you show me how cooperative you can be?"

(*Not* "You never let me give you a bath.")

"If you undress yourself, I'll give you one point. And pretty soon, when you have ten points, I'll let you trade them for a special present."

(*Not* "You're so difficult to undress.")

Focus on the task at hand instead of spending time and energy criticizing your child. If you do, your child will be more cooperative, and you'll feel better about your skills as a parent.

I don't want to imply that mere positivism is a magical cure for every ill. But it is a powerful tool. In every situation you have a choice: to react positively (and reinforce your child's self-esteem) or negatively (and hurt it).

If you begin following the principles in this chapter now—if you let your child learn at his own pace, if you praise him regularly, if, instead of criticizing him, you focus on the positive—your child's self-image will develop wonderfully right from the start.

SUMMARY

Let your child learn at his own pace. Give him time to figure things out for himself.

Praise your child in every way you can (not just with words, but with rewards, cuddling, rocking).

Focus on her efforts and achievements; it's too early to worry about her failures.

Leave criticism out of it. If you want your child to do something right, tell him *that*—not that he did it wrong the last time.

2

▀▄

THE POWER OF
POSITIVE REINFORCEMENT

CHARLIE'S STORY

Charlie, a bright-eyed five-year-old, was experiencing his first
prolonged exposure to the "outside world"—a small kindergar-
ten just a few blocks from his house. There was no reason for
Charlie to feel insecure there, but he did. His teachers noticed
that he seemed uncertain around his classmates; his parents
observed that he was usually content to play by himself while
other children made new friends.

Charlie looked unhappy. And that made his parents *miserable.*

Charlie's parents wanted him to be happy. When they told me
about their son, I suggested they could do a lot to help him just
by giving him positive reinforcement. (Even on their own, they
had observed that children who received healthy doses of praise
seemed more self-assured, more adaptable, and more adventur-
ous than those who didn't.)

But what was there to praise, they wondered? Charlie was

smart, but not unusually smart. He was cute, but no cuter than most of the five-year-olds his parents saw. He wasn't as verbal as many of his peers, or as coordinated. He was an *okay* kid—not some "superstar child" who deserved lavish paeans.

As we talked, Charlie's parents realized they couldn't keep waiting until they had something special to praise, or they might wait forever. I encouraged them to start praising him right away. I suggested that:

They praise him *no matter what.*
They make praising him a habit.
They actively *seek out* things to praise.

- So what if he wasn't the most popular kid in his school? Didn't his efforts to make friends deserve their recognition?
- So what if he wasn't the best athlete on the block? Wasn't the energy with which he worked at learning sports impressive?
- So what if he didn't show signs of having a mega-IQ? Wasn't he learning new words every day?

Charlie's parents saw my point, and they began praising him—first once, then twice, then three times a day. At first they had to remind themselves with notes on their desks ("PRAISE CHARLIE NOW!") and in their wallets ("COMPLIMENT CHARLIE THIS MINUTE!"). Soon they didn't need reminders—praising Charlie had become a habit.

Compliments, once rare, became regular events. After all, small acts, little efforts worthy of praise, presented themselves all the time. (They had always presented themselves. But until now, Charlie's parents hadn't noticed.)

They didn't tell Charlie he was the smartest kid in the world. (He wouldn't have believed that, anyway.) They looked for little things to praise ("I love the way you used red in this painting."), or they praised attempts ("It was terrific the way you tried to catch that ball."—although he dropped it).

In time . . .

They learned to praise the effort—no matter what they thought of the result. "It was great to see you trying so hard."

They learned to praise the small. "You did a great job brushing your teeth this morning." (Never mind that he got toothpaste on the floor.)

They learned to praise specific acts. "I really liked the way you helped me fold the laundry."

And they looked for things to praise in Charlie's weakest area, making new friends. Every time he took even a small step in the right direction, they came through with positive reinforcement. "It was so nice of you to talk to the new girl in your class today." "You were so friendly to the boy who moved in down the block."

Here are some of the compliments Charlie's parents gave him:

Day One

8:00 A.M.	It's so nice when you get out of bed on time.
12:10 P.M.	I hear you were such a good friend to Liza today. Terrific.
12:17	It's wonderful of you to tell me all about what you did in school.
12:30	I like the way you handled that situation in the sandbox.
1:40	It was very considerate of you to keep me company.
3:20	You were so patient with your little brother today; I know it's hard sometimes.
7:15	I like your hair.
8:00	You got undressed all by yourself. Bravo!

Day Two

8:07 A.M.	It's great that you got dressed yourself.
12:15 P.M.	It's really nice of you to help me make your sandwich.
12:19	I've really enjoyed spending this time talking to you.
1:15	It was fun pushing you on the swing today. I loved hearing you laugh.
2:30	That's a great city you built from blocks.
4:57	Your smile is beautiful.
5:20	I appreciate your kindness to Grandpa.
7:30	You folded up your clothes so well.

Day Three

8:20 A.M.	It was so nice of you to hold your brother's hand on the way to school.
12:16 P.M.	It was really helpful of you to get the glass out of the cabinet.
12:40	It's great that you were so friendly to that new boy.
12:50	I think Erica really liked the way you played with her.
2:10	It was thoughtful of you to not interrupt me when I was on the phone.
2:20	It was nice to hear you sing.
4:00	You worked hard hammering that nail. I'm proud of you.
5:50	It's really great when you bring home a painting that you made.

Didn't all the praise go right to Charlie's head? You bet! Gradually Charlie began to believe what he was hearing. His parents' praise made him feel, "I'm a good person. I'm worthy of love." And soon his behavior reflected his new feelings: he seemed more comfortable making new friends, trying new things, mastering new situations.

▼▲

If you're a parent, you already know how to criticize.

Even if you're a wonderful parent, you probably criticize too much. From time to time, I've asked parents to keep track of how often they criticize their children. The answers have ranged from twenty to fifty to one hundred times *a day*.

You're probably not that bad. But, then again, when it comes to criticizing your child, you've got help— professional help. According to one researcher, 87 percent of what teachers tell children in the classroom is negative. Another researcher found that "students encounter the equivalent of sixty days each year of reprimanding, nagging, and punishment. During twelve years of schooling, a student is subject to 15,000 negative statements." (And that's despite the fact that children learn better when praise is used to motivate them.)

Then there are your child's friends. If you've ever eavesdropped on playground conversation, you know how cutting it can be:

"You're stupid."
"You're the ugliest girl in the neighborhood."
"You're a rotten friend."

How does all that criticism make your child feel?

It seems like I do everything wrong. I'm such a dumb kid. No wonder you don't love me. You don't even like me. And why should you? I'm nothing.

Irrational? Perhaps. But that's how criticism may sound to your child.

Of course you don't like criticizing your child. You hate to hear yourself nagging or finding fault. You criticize because it's easy, because you're tired and overworked, and because it's natural to focus on the bad. (Problems tend to get our attention; they're inconvenient and disruptive. It's hard to ignore your child when he's broken a rule or made a mess.)

Sometimes you criticize because you want to change your child's behavior. But your "constructive criticism" is probably more *destructive* than you realize.

Cutting the criticism

1. Every day for a week, keep track of how many times you criticize your child.
2. Calculate your average number of criticisms per day.
3. Try to cut out one criticism each day, until you're down to zero.

Say you criticize your child an average of ten times a day. On the first day of this "program," try to cut down to nine. On the second day, aim for eight. And so on.

Of course it's hard to be that precise about how many times you criticize your child. But it's still a good idea to count. Because I think you'll find that if you focus on how many criticisms you give, you'll automatically cut back. *Once you realize just what you've been doing, you'll want to stop.*

Criticizing your child less often is a first step toward improving her self-image. But it's only half the battle. After you've stopped criticizing your child, you'll need to learn to fill the "dead air time" with praise. *Imagine how good your child will feel if you begin giving out compliments as freely as Charlie's parents did.*

When it comes to praising your child, you may experience these problems:

You don't know what to praise. For every act worthy of praise, you'll notice ten worthy of criticism.

You don't know how to praise. No school teaches you how to give compliments, and even the best parenting guides stop short of giving you specific instructions on how to praise—though praise may be the greatest gift you can give your child.

Praising little things feels "funny." At first you'll feel silly commenting on things that seem minute, almost invisible. When you think about it, though, your child's faults and mistakes are really petty—much more so than the strengths and achievements you've been overlooking.

Learning to give praise takes work. If it doesn't come naturally, that may be because we haven't heard enough compliments ourselves. In many cases, our own parents were stingy with praise. *But we want to do better.*

Learning to praise your child will take practice, patience, and a sense of humor. As you follow the steps in this chapter, you won't be able to do everything right the first time. That's okay— you'll get better with practice.

As you start to replace criticism with praise, you may ask yourself these questions:

Can't my child develop a good self-image on his own, without positive reinforcement?

That's like asking, "Can't my child learn to speak without hearing anyone talk?" Self-image is learned. Before he can think positive things about himself, your child needs to hear those things from others.

Won't my child think it's strange if I start to praise him all the time?

Not really. We don't question why the sun is shining—we just enjoy it. In the same way, your child won't say, "Why did you stop criticizing me?" He'll just bask in the praise.

Besides, if your child will think it's strange for you to praise him, that's all the more reason to start.

Shouldn't I be using praise to change my child's behavior?

Praise a behavior you like (cleanliness, politeness) and your child may exhibit it more often. However, the main thrust of this book isn't to correct bad behavior, it's to enhance self-esteem. But over time, improving self-esteem will change behavior in the best way possible: that is, your child will act better because he feels better about himself.

In my practice I have treated hundreds of children with social and psychological problems. In many cases, even some of the most severe ones, a steady regimen of positive reinforcement was the most effective treatment. Praise is a very powerful tool.

Lynn, nine, complained of stomach aches every morning before she left for school. The real problem was that she felt inadequate and stupid—though it was clear to me she wasn't. I asked her parents, who were part of the problem, to become part of the solution. How? I had them eliminate the word *wrong* from their vocabulary and substitute *great try.* Once criticism gave way to praise, Lynn blossomed.

Steve, a friendly ten-year-old, was smart, but denied it, and was good looking, but denied that too. I got the whole class involved in improving his self-image (though they didn't know that's what they were doing). The teacher put up mailboxes in the back of the room and the kids were taught to leave each other complimentary notes. After reading enough "Praise-grams," Steve started to believe good things about himself. At the principal's request, the whole school adopted the mailbox system.

James, seven, threw temper tantrums. The problem was that he didn't feel comfortable expressing what he felt through normal channels. I taught his parents to praise him whenever he expressed honest feelings—*whether they agreed with those feelings or not.* Slowly, James began to have an easier time expressing feelings and he began to relax about himself. Within six months, his negative behavior had subsided.

Erica, eight, endured regular put-downs from her parents. When they counted, her parents found they criticized her forty to fifty times a day. Not surprisingly, when I asked her to list three things she liked about herself, she couldn't come up with *one.* And since she was a mediocre student, her high-achieving parents said they couldn't find a thing to praise.

I taught Erica's parents how to scan her schoolwork and find something to compliment—no matter what. Pretty soon they could look at a report and find something to praise, as if by instinct. ("Look. Your penmanship is so much better." "Boy, it's great how much effort you put into this." "That first sentence really explains the subject well.")

One day Erica brought home a paper from school for one of her parents to sign. On the top of the paper, the teacher had written "−65." Erica's father wrote "+35" in big red letters. Then he signed the paper and sent it back.

Raymond, eleven, seemed to be in competition with his father—but his father had the upper hand. (Jack was forever demonstrating his superior knowledge of sports in ways that made Raymond feel stupid.) I asked Raymond and Jack to take turns asking each other very hard sports trivia questions. If Raymond came up with a wrong answer, Jack would say, "Nice try. You came very close." Raymond would do the same for Jack. And though it was just a game, it did wonders for Raymond's self-image (and Jack's).

Praise your child four times a day—or more.

You can start by giving her one or two compliments a day; then gradually work your way up to four. Your spouse should do the same. If you're a single parent, try to work up to five or six compliments a day. Or maybe you can get someone to help (a grandparent, a friend, a lover). But if you can only manage four compliments a day, that's fine. *That's four more compliments than your child is getting now.*

Should you compliment your child twenty or fifty or one hundred times a day? Probably not. If you praise your child that often, your compliments may lose their meaning.

Praise as many different aspects of your child's behavior as you can.

To have the maximum impact on your child's self-image, compliment as many different things as you can think of, from the color of his socks to how fast he jumped out of bed in the morning to the colors in his latest fingerpainting.

Try to compliment your child in each of these areas:

Social skills
Appearance
Expressiveness
Intelligence
Coordination
Cooperativeness

Be concrete and specific.

Especially at the beginning of the process, look for specific actions to praise ("You were so good at checkers today."). Until a child feels really good about himself, he won't be able to accept a "global" compliment ("You're great!") without discounting it. But if you compliment a specific action, he'll believe you. He can't deny that he just cleaned his room or cleared the table.

Be genuine.

Mean what you say. Children have a knack for distinguishing the real from the artificial. And hypocrisy turns them off. So don't fake it. Even a very small compliment ("I like the bow in your hair.") is better than a lie ("You've never looked more gorgeous.").

Praise the effort.

Try to forget about results; instead, compliment your child for trying. *Not* "It's wonderful that you got all the answers right," *but* "You worked really hard studying for that test. I'm proud."

"That's wonderful. You almost made it."
"You came really close. Terrific."
"Hurrah. That's the best you've ever done."

Avoid pressure compliments.

"I know you're capable of getting an A on the next test." That's telling her *what she should do* instead of praising *what she's done.* Besides, there's no better way to set her up for disappointment.

"I know you're a good enough runner to win the race." That may be a terrific strategy if you're a coach, but it does nothing for her self-image.

Avoid left-handed compliments.

The idea is to praise, not to correct.
Omit the words in brackets:
"You spoke so nicely to Grandpa. [But I wish you had also called Grandma.]"

"It's great that you got home from school so quickly. [But why didn't you clean your room?]"

Concentrate on your child's area of greatest weakness.

Praise wherever praise will do the most good.

If his coordination is poor:

"You went up the stairs really quickly. Congratulations."
"You did really well riding your bike today; that's hard to do."

If she's shy:

"I loved listening to you read to me just now."
"I was so proud that you asked the librarian for help finding that book."

If he's having trouble with schoolwork:

"It sounds like you really tried hard in school today."
"It was great that you were able to get so many math problems right today."

If he's unassertive:

"I'm glad you said what you felt."
"I think it's great that you spoke up when Jeff wanted to go to the movies and you didn't."

If she's generally uncooperative or unhelpful:

"It was very nice of you to carry your dishes to the sink."
"You were great to play with your dolls while I was getting ready."
"I appreciate your putting away all those crayons."
"It was really nice of you to hold your little sister for a while."

If he's fidgety or hyperactive:

"It was very considerate of you to wait for me so patiently."
"It was nice of you to be so quiet while the doctor examined you."
"I enjoyed your sitting with me for that quiet chat just now."

If he's easily scared:

"It was very brave of you to do something so difficult."

"You were so mature when the power went off; it helped me keep a cool head."

Make the best of a bad situation.

"It took a lot of courage to say something so difficult to me."

"You're doing great for someone who's so angry."

Learn to scan your child's work.

When your child brings home a book report, or a picture he painted in class, try to find something to praise instantly—*even if you don't like the whole thing.*

"Wow. I like this little figure on the left."

(*Not* "What's this painting supposed to be?")

"I see a very difficult word you spelled correctly."

(*Not* "Let me read this, and I'll tell you what I think.")

Avoid hyperbole.

"You're the greatest kid in the world."

"You're the smartest kid in town."

(This isn't real praise; it's pabulum. And your child will sense that.)

Be resourceful.

Sometimes it can be hard to find something to praise.

If you do have trouble, don't worry: look back at Charlie's parents' list on pages 31–32. Or think about what you're inclined to criticize, and look for the flip side.

If you're thinking, "You didn't do very well on this report," say, "You tried real hard on this report."

Instead of, "You were supposed to be home twenty minutes ago," say, "You were a good friend to stay and help James with his homework."

Feel free to praise in writing.

At first you may find it easier to write compliments than to speak them. That's fine. In fact, if you leave your child a note, he can savor it for days.

- Put a little note in his lunchbox: "You have a beautiful smile."
- Tape a note onto the bathroom mirror: "Hi, Alexandra, you have such a pretty face."
- Leave a short letter on his desk: "Your idea of bringing flowers to Grandma on Sunday was so thoughtful and caring. We are lucky to have a son like you. Signed, Your Proud Parents."

Surprise your child.

Try not to be too predictable. If your child always knows when you're about to praise him, your praise may lose its meaning. Whenever you can, let praise sneak up on him when he least expects it.

Speaking of which, here's some praise for you:

You obviously care a lot about your child.

You've made a real effort to learn the rules for giving praise.

Your children are lucky to have you as a parent.

It's terrific that you bought this book. It shows a real commitment to your child's well-being.

You deserve a lot of admiration for trying out the techniques in this book. That means you're committed, energetic, and loving. Congratulations.

SUMMARY

Give your child at least four compliments a day (but not fifty or one hundred)—in as many different areas as you can.

Be concrete and specific. (Don't say, "You're the smartest kid in the world." He won't believe it. Do say, "It was really nice of you to clear the table." He can't deny that.)

Praise small things. "You put your mittens on by yourself; that's terrific."

Don't give pressure compliments. ("I'm sure you're smart enough to get an A on tomorrow's test.")

Don't give left-handed compliments. ("You're doing great in math; now maybe you'll do better in English.")

Find things to praise in your child's weakest area (the area where praise will do the most good).

Find the best in a bad situation. ("It took a lot of courage for you to tell your teacher why your homework wasn't done.")

Don't be predictable; surprise your child with unexpected praise.

3

▀▀

THE QUESTION:
"TELL ME SOMETHING
YOU LIKE ABOUT YOURSELF"

KAREN'S STORY

Karen's parents were afraid their daughter was developing a low self-image, and that scared them. They had hoped she would be confident and self-assured—but at six she already seemed timid and withdrawn. When she talked about herself, she said things like, "I'm a bad girl," "I'm stupid," and "No one wants me to come to the party." And when she compared herself to other children, she usually came up short: Other children, she was starting to notice, were prettier. Other children lived in bigger houses, or had more friends—and, to her, that made them better.

Karen's parents knew that a low self-image could turn into a lifelong handicap for Karen. At a meeting in my office, they asked what they could do to help her.

Naturally I suggested that they praise their daughter every day (chapter 1), and I showed them how to do that. Praise, I said, would serve to remind Karen that there were lots of things to like about her. But Karen needed even more than a reminder. Our goal, I said, would be to shift Karen's attention from her shortcomings (which she seemed to think about all the time) to her strengths (which she ignored). The way to do that, I said, was to ask her The Question—"Tell me something you like about yourself"—every day. I talked to Karen's parents about ways to ask The Question gently but meaningfully, and about ways to help Karen respond. Then I asked *them* The Question, and I worked with them until they were comfortable answering it. (After all, they would have to serve as role models for Karen.) The first time I asked Karen's parents The Question, they didn't answer. (Like their daughter, they were uncomfortable talking about their strengths.) But, before the end of our first session, we had this exchange:

ME: *(To Karen's mother)* Can you tell me something you like about yourself.
KAREN'S MOTHER: Yeah, I feel good about the fact that I'm making this effort to help Karen.
ME: Terrific.
ME: *(To Karen's father)* Is there something you like about yourself?
KAREN'S FATHER: Sure. I feel proud of the fact that I have such a good marriage.
ME: Great.

Karen's parents were enthusiastic about my approach, and I was confident they could do a lot to help their daughter.

The next morning, without fanfare, Karen's father turned to her at breakfast and said, "Karen, can you tell me something you like about yourself?" Karen looked confused, so he asked again.

"Karen, I'd love to know something you like about yourself."
Karen didn't answer. She was unaccustomed to thinking (much
less talking) about her strengths. She was probably wondering,
"How could I like anything about myself?" Karen's parents
understood that, and they didn't push her. But they didn't give
up, either. The next day Karen's mother asked her The Question, and this time she suggested answers:

"Did you like the way you helped Carl with his puzzle?"
"Did you feel good about being so nice to Grandma?"
"Do you like the way you look in that new dress?"

Karen didn't answer. She still felt strange talking about her
strengths. Her parents knew that, and they began asking each
other The Question in front of Karen, to show her that answering The Question wasn't as hard as Karen thought.

MOTHER: Tell me something you like about yourself.
FATHER: Let's see. I like the fact that I'm nice to the people in
my office. Now, could you tell me something you like about
yourself?
MOTHER: I like the fact that I am learning to speak French.

Soon they were asking each other The Question once or twice
a day. Karen noticed that they actually seemed to *enjoy* answering The Question.

Karen thought maybe, just maybe, she would answer the
Question soon. But what would she say? She wasn't gorgeous,
or brilliant, or talented. Karen's parents sensed her self-doubt,
and they began praising her (to boost her self-esteem as well as
to suggest possible answers to The Question).

"Karen, your eyes sparkle so beautifully."

"Your teacher said you're getting along so well with your classmates. We're really glad to hear that."

"Karen, I just wanted to tell you that you're a patient, loyal friend to Jenny, and I'm proud of you for that."

Then Karen's parents began to ask her The Question in ways that didn't overwhelm her:

"Tell me something you did today that you *felt good about.*"

"Tell me something you *feel you did well* today."

"Tell me something you *enjoyed* today."

"Tell me something you *liked about yourself* today."

And again they praised her.

Three days after they first asked her The Question, Karen said, "I loved playing kickball *today.*" In the next few days, she said, "I loved school *today*" and "I made a new friend *today.*"

She wasn't ready to describe herself in glowing terms ("I'm a great person."), but she was able to talk about things she'd done that felt good. And that was a very big step for Karen.

Gradually her parents switched to more general versions of The Question. And gradually Karen became comfortable enough to answer them. Here are some of the answers she came up with in the next few weeks:

"I like the fact that when I make a friend, I stick with her."

"I like helping my younger brother build sand castles."

"I like my red hair."

"I like knowing I've kept my room clean."

Soon, Karen's parents were asking her The Question every day, and Karen was responding confidently. (Sometimes she used the same answers over and over, but that didn't matter. The important thing was that she was becoming comfortable talking about her strengths.)

Then, gradually, Karen began to "hear" what she was saying. After answering The Question over and over, she began to think of herself as a competent, worthwhile person. Her words were starting to sink in.

Karen's parents began to see an improvement in Karen's self-image. She had stopped saying bad things about herself, and she often described herself in a favorable light.

Of course, Karen's parents didn't stop asking her The Question. In fact, they said, they planned to keep asking Karen The Question "forever."

I spoke to them just before Karen's seventh birthday. They told me their daughter was more sure of herself, more confident, more positive than ever. "And all that," said her parents, "from a simple question."

▼▲

If you're like most parents, you ask your child lots of different questions.

But you probably don't get lots of different answers.

"What did you do in school today?"
"Nothing."

"What are you thinking about?"
"Nothing."

"What's new?"
"Nothing."

"What are you planning for this weekend?"
"Nothing."

Instead, why not try asking The Question—"Tell me something you like about yourself."

By asking your child The Question, you will

1. *Learn about the state of your child's self-image.*
Most children can't answer The Question the first time they hear it. (To answer The Question the first time requires an unusually strong self-image.)

But most children can *learn* to answer The Question. As your child's self-image improves, his ability to answer The Question will improve with it.

By asking your child The Question regularly as you work your way through this book, you will be "monitoring" the state of his self-image.

2. *Focus your child's attention on his successes.*
Most of us have no problem talking about our failures.

"I'll never learn to do this right."
"I could kick myself for forgetting his name again."
"I totally botched that meeting. No one in there respects me."

But when we have to talk about our successes, we clam up. We feel uncomfortable, immodest, insecure.

Your child is no different. She has good qualities, but she may never talk about them. She probably doesn't even like to think about them.

But The Question can change that. By asking her The Question, Karen's parents were able to focus her attention on her strengths—and the impact on her behavior was dramatic. You can do the same thing for your child.

Here's how:

Ask your child The Question at least once a day.

"Adrian, there's a question I want to ask you. Can you tell me something you like about yourself?"

You don't need to explain why you're asking The Question. But if your child asks, tell him the truth: "I'm asking you because I love you, and if there's something you like about yourself, I'd love to hear about it."

Chances are, your child won't be able to answer The Question immediately. If he can, congratulations. You've been doing something right.

If he can't, don't worry. You can teach your child to answer The Question, probably in less than a week. That's what this chapter's about.

To make it easier for your child, you may want to start off with these less intimidating versions of The Question:

"Tell me something you liked about yourself *today.*"
"Tell me something you felt good about *today.*"
"Tell me something you think you did well *today.*"

For a child who has difficulty with those, try:

"Tell me something you *enjoyed* today."

Or you may want to zero in on specific activities:

"Tell me what you felt good about when you were playing with your friends."
"Was there anything you liked when you were doing your homework?"

Praise your child often, in order to suggest possible answers to The Question.

MOTHER: I think your hair looks beautiful after you've washed it. Now, can you tell me something you like about yourself?
CHILD: I think my hair looks beautiful after I've washed it.
MOTHER: Terrific.

Don't worry if your child simply repeats a compliment you just gave her. The idea is for her to become accustomed to talking about her strengths, even if she has to mimic you to do so.

Show your child that a "small" response is okay.
If he says, "I liked the way I tried to hit the ball in gym class," that's enough for now. (It doesn't have to be, "I'm the best athlete in the school.")

Show your child that an attempt is okay.
Help him say, "I'm glad I tried so hard in art class." (It doesn't have to be, "I painted a masterpiece.")

Show your child that an improvement is okay.
"I'm glad I'm doing my times tables faster than I did them last week." (It doesn't have to be, "I have all my times tables down cold.")

"I got one hard word right today." (It doesn't have to be, "I won the spelling bee in school today.")

"I tried to answer a hard question in geography today." (It doesn't have to be, "I got every question right.")

"I talked to George at recess." (It doesn't have to be, "I made five new friends.")

To be able to answer The Question, your child doesn't have to be the best at anything. All he has to be is himself.

Learn to weave The Question into your everyday routine.

A good time to ask your child The Question is when he comes home from school. Instead of, "What did you do in school today?"—every parent's throwaway question—ask something that matters: "What did you enjoy in school today?" "What did you feel good about in math class?"

At the dinner table, show your child how well *you* answer The Question.

MOTHER: *(To Father)* Can you tell me something you like about yourself?
FATHER: Sure. I didn't lose my temper on the highway today when a guy stopped short in front of me, and I'm proud of that.

(He didn't say, "I was the best driver on the road." Instead, he noted a small accomplishment.)

FATHER: How about you? Can you tell me something you liked about yourself today?
MOTHER: I asked for a promotion today, and I feel great that I was able to do that.

(She didn't say, "I was made president of the company today."
Instead, she focused on an attempt.)

If you don't have a spouse to help you, try to enlist a friend.
Or you can answer the question "solo":

MOM: Jessica, I want to tell you about something I feel good
about. This afternoon, I stopped by the nursing home to see
Great Uncle Ralph. I felt good about taking time out of my day
to do that.

By answering The Question yourself, you will be showing your
child what to do *and* reducing her anxiety about doing it.

Warning: Don't answer The Question by one-upping: "When
I was your age, I got straight A's." "I've always had wonderful
relationships with all my friends." Frankly, statements like that
may be part of the problem. How can a child hope to keep up
with parents who are perfect?

Make answering The Question fun.

At bedtime, try the trading game: "I'll tell you something I
like about myself; you tell me something you like about yourself."

Use multiple choice.

Did you feel good about . . .

- what you did in art class today?
- what you did in gym?
- helping your teacher hand out papers in homeroom?

What did you like about the way you . . .

- played with your friends today?
- helped me make dinner?
- got dressed all by yourself this morning?

When multiple choice isn't enough, make your questions even more specific.

"You helped Molly hand out snacks today. Did you feel good about that?"

"I love your drawing. How do you feel about it?"

"You tied your shoelaces all by yourself. Do you feel pleased?"

But don't second-guess.

YOU: I see you got a letter from Amanda. You should feel good about that. Don't you?

CHILD: No. I hope I never speak to her again.

(After all, this is a *question.* The goal is for you to find out what your child is feeling—not to tell him what he *should* feel.)

Use positive reinforcement.

Praise your child for answering The Question.

"I'm so glad you told me that."

"Thank you for telling me about that."

"I really liked hearing about those feelings."

Make answering The Question a game.

For the reluctant child, for the shy child, for the uncooperative child, words of praise may not be enough. You may want to offer her concrete and tangible rewards. For example, reward your child with an extra story at bedtime, or some one-on-one soccer practice, or an afternoon at the beach for answering The Question. Or give out points. And tell your child that enough points will earn him a specific reward: you'll build a new model airplane together, or you'll take him skating, or you'll cook his favorite dinner!

Create variants on The Question geared to your child's situation.

For a child suffering from shyness on the playground:

"How did it feel to play with that nice boy, Steven?"
"You went over and talked to Susan. Are you glad you did that?"

For a child who's afraid to be alone:

"You were up in your room by yourself for almost an hour. Are you proud of yourself?"

Ask your child versions of The Question that relate to a particular problem he's having. The power of The Question—to help him focus on desirable behaviors—may astonish you.

Jeff, six, was having difficulty with friends; his extreme aggressiveness alienated other children.
Questions:

"What game did you enjoy the most today?"
"Did you feel good about playing with David today?"

"Is there anything you liked about playing with Steven?"

"How do you feel about your new friendship with Rachel?"

David, nine, had trouble being assertive.

Questions:

"Did you feel good about making your opinion known in class today?"

"When you told Mark how to handle that problem, did you feel good?"

"How did it feel when you volunteered to be the magician's assistant?"

Lynn, eight, had a school phobia; she was often depressed and was not participating in class.

Questions:

"Did you feel good about volunteering in English class today?"

"What did you enjoy about walking to school today with Arthur?"

Catherine, ten, was extremely sensitive to rejection; if a teacher didn't give her immediate attention, she felt it was because the teacher didn't like her.

Questions:

"Did you feel good about getting a part in the school play?"

"How did it feel when you didn't get upset because Mr. Truby didn't call on you?"

Jenny, seven, had protruding teeth—which caused her to hate her looks.

Questions:

"Did you like the way you looked in your new skirt today?"
"Which of your outfits do you think you look the best in?"
"Did you like having your hair in a ponytail this week?"

Getting your child to answer The Question may not be as easy as you'd like. You will almost certainly have to help him along with encouragement and positive reinforcement—"I know it's hard to answer. But I feel you're really trying, and that's great."

But before you get discouraged, think about how good you'll feel when your child answers The Question for the first time (or the hundredth).

One more thing: Don't stop asking The Question. It should remain in your parenting repertoire forever.

SUMMARY

Ask your child The Question—"Tell me something you like about yourself"—at least once a day.

If your child has a hard time answering The Question, start with:

"Tell me something you liked about yourself *today.*"
"Tell me something you felt good about *today.*"
"Tell me something you think you *did well* today."
"Tell me something you *enjoyed* today."

Show your child that a small response is okay. ("I brushed my own teeth.")

Show your child that an attempt is okay. ("I tried real hard to win.")

Show your child that an improvement is okay. ("I did that better than the last time.")

Give a reluctant child a multiple-choice version of The Question. ("Did you feel good about . . . ?" "How about . . . ?")

Show your child how well you answer The Question (by exchanging answers with a partner).

Weave The Question into your everyday routine. (After school: "Tell me something you did well today.")

Praise your child (as a way of suggesting possible answers to The Question).

Praise your child again for answering The Question (or for simply trying). You may also want to offer tangible rewards for answering The Question.

4

▚▚

THE GIFT OF
EMPATHY

JASON'S STORY

Until he was four, Jason rarely spoke. Now, at seven, he was hardly ever quiet. He talked all the time. Yet he had a hard time communicating what was on his mind. His "rap" was a combination of unfinished thoughts and run-on sentences. His friends found him annoying. His teachers had a hard time figuring out how much he was learning—because he couldn't tell them. His four older brothers and sisters (all highly verbal) made fun of Jason when he tried to talk.

Yet there was nothing funny about Jason's plight. He was *trying* to express himself. He had feelings—lots of feelings—about school, friends, growing up—but when he tried to tell people about them, he got nowhere.

Jason was frustrated. And that wasn't likely to change. As the littlest member of the family, he was often overlooked. When Jason tried to talk to them, his parents watched TV, paid bills, read magazines, or wrote letters; they rarely *just* listened.

Busy as they were, Jason's parents were aware of his situation. They knew that, as their youngest child, he had received the least attention. And though their time was limited, they wanted to make sure that he developed as successfully as his older siblings. Jason's parents came to see me. They told me about Jason, and they asked if I could help him.

I responded by saying that I could help Jason, but to do that I would have to work with *them*. The idea, I explained, was to teach them to empathize with Jason. Once they learned to empathize with Jason, I said, he would feel comfortable expressing feelings, and that would make him feel worthy, important. Both his verbal ability and his self-image would improve.

Jason's parents were surprised by my approach. After all, they were nice people—weren't they already empathetic? I explained that there's more to empathy than simply being nice. Empathy is a specific skill—and one that most of us have never learned, because no one has taught it to us.

This is the definition of empathy I gave to Jason's parents:

- Putting yourself in another person's place, and feeling his feelings.
- Caring about that person's feelings—even the feelings you disagree with.
- Letting the person know you care.

Jason's parents agreed to work with me, and I told them I would teach them empathy in four stages.

Stage One

At our first meeting, I asked them to try to listen to Jason for at least one ten-minute period each day. During "listening times" they couldn't talk on the phone, watch TV, read, or concentrate on anything but Jason.

To keep the conversation going, they could say, "That's great." "Really?" "No kidding?" "That's interesting. Tell me more." But they couldn't approve, disapprove, change the subject, or in any way inject their opinions into the conversation. And they had to *look* like they were listening. I asked them to face Jason, making direct eye contact, and to smile or nod every few seconds.

When I spoke to them again a few days later, Jason's parents told me that listening—just listening—was one of the hardest things they'd ever done. They hadn't realized how little actual listening they had done before. Sure, Jason had talked for ten minutes at a time, and they had listened to *some* of what he said. But they had never listened to him for ten minutes at a time— until now.

Stage Two

I asked Jason's parents to keep listening to him—and, from time to time, to repeat what he was saying. The idea was to let him know that they were paying close attention to his thoughts and feelings. I warned them that at first repeating might feel awkward. But, I said, it would quickly become second nature.

Then we practiced. I played Jason's role.

ME (as Jason): I'm so mad at the moon.
DAD: How can you be mad at the moon?
ME: No. Try to repeat what I said.
DAD: Okay. You're mad at the moon.
ME: Terrific.

When they got home, Jason's parents practiced repeating what he said. Their conversations went like this:

JASON: I'm so mad. I'm so, so mad. The refrigerator door hit me.
MOM: You're mad that the refrigerator hit you.
JASON: I want a dog. I want a lot of dogs. I want one hundred dogs.
DAD: You want one hundred dogs.

Were Jason's parents being permissive or indulgent? Not at all. They were simply making him feel that what he said was important to them.

Did Jason think his parents were being silly? Hardly. When he talked, he knew he was being listened to. And, already, his parents noticed that he was speaking more calmly, more comfortably. He didn't need to blurt out all his thoughts at once. He could speak carefully and slowly, because he didn't have to fight for his parents' attention.

Stage Three

The next time I saw Jason's parents, I asked them to keep listening to Jason, to keep repeating what he was saying, and to tell him—at regular intervals—that they *understood* what he was saying. (They didn't always have to like it or agree with it. All they had to do was understand it.)

They told me they would try; their conversations during the next few days went like this:

JASON: I've never been so angry. I'm angry at you. I'm angry.
MOM: I can understand your being angry. [She didn't think he had much of a reason to be angry, but she understood how he felt.]

JASON: I hate Margie.
DAD: I understand you hate Margie. [He liked Margie, Jason's babysitter, but he understood that at this moment, Jason didn't.]

By now, Jason's parents felt they were becoming empathetic parents. They were listening to what Jason said and making sure *he knew* that they were listening. And they were letting him know that they understood his feelings (whether they agreed with those feelings or not).

Stage Four

At our next meeting, I asked Jason's parents to continue listening to Jason and to *paraphrase* what he was saying, telling him *in their own words* that they could understand his feelings.
I asked them:

- not to disagree with him.
- not to try to solve whatever problem he was having. (Not yet.)
- not to correct him, or help him speak.
- not to express *their* feelings. (Again, not yet.)

What I wanted them to do was to empathize with Jason.
Here are two of their conversations:

JASON: I'm as tired as anybody in the world.
MOM: I can understand that you're exhausted after such a long day.

JASON: I don't ever want to see you again.
DAD: I can understand that you'd be angry at me after what happened today. I'm sorry you feel that way.

Jason's parents had begun teaching his brothers and sisters how to give empathy, and they were getting better and better at it. The entire family was becoming empathetic. By now, when Jason spoke, he could expect someone to seem interested, to pay attention. His parents (and siblings) no longer changed the subject, watched TV, or made him feel that his ideas were worthless.

Jason, in turn, was expressing feelings competently and clearly. And, because he knew his feelings were worthwhile, his self-image was improving. He was expressing more positives about himself. He compared himself favorably to other children. He had a newfound sense of being competent and in control.

Although Jason's parents were only spending a few more minutes a day with him, they no longer felt that they were ignoring their son. They were using their time together—limited as it was—to make Jason feel wanted and important.

▀▀

To empathize with your child is one of the most important things you can do as a parent. By empathizing, you will teach him that what he feels is important—and, by extension, that *he's* important. And that will have a direct effect on his self-image.

To empathize with your child means:

■ to try to understand your child's feeling (to put yourself in his shoes).

■ to care about your child's feeling.

■ to express that caring—unambiguously, fully. (It's not enough to care if you don't show it.)

■ to hold off on voicing disapproval or disagreement. (If you must disagree, do so *later.*)

You may not know how to be empathetic—like most parents, you've probably never been taught. But by failing to empathize with your child, you are (unknowingly) sending your child a message: that his feelings are not important. You are (unintentionally) putting your child down. By cutting him off, ignoring him, or disagreeing with him, you may be preventing him from developing a strong self-image.

Empathy is a skill you can learn.

Once you have learned it, your expressions of empathy will heighten your child's feelings of being understood, loved, and accepted.

Sorry: love isn't enough.

No doubt you love your child, and you express your love in all sorts of ways (by telling him you love him, by providing a safe, comfortable environment, by giving him physical affection, by giving him gifts). Don't stop doing any of those things—they're all important. But expressing love in those ways—crucial as they are—may not have a specific effect on your child's self-image.

I've worked with many low-self-esteem children whose parents love them very much. Love alone isn't enough to give a child a strong self-image.

Empathy, on the other hand, is a way of expressing love that will have a *direct impact on your child's self-image.* By empathizing, you are sending your child a clear-cut message that he's an important, worthwhile, and valuable person.

I've heard parents of low-self-image children say, "But I've given my child everything." And they have. But "everything"

probably didn't include empathy. (Indeed, "everything" probably wasn't as important—or as inexpensive.)

To give empathy isn't as easy as it sounds. Like Jason's parents, you may be shocked to discover how little empathy you've
been giving your child.

There are four steps to giving empathy. You can probably
learn them in about a month. But no one is watching you
or grading you. So do as much as you can, when you can, being careful to master each stage before going on to the next
one.

At first the techniques for giving empathy may seem contrived
or arbitrary. Many new skills feel that way at first. But that
feeling won't last. After a while you won't have to think before
you empathize; you'll just do it automatically (and you'll feel
great every time you do).

1. Listen.

The first (and possibly the most important) part of giving
empathy is to listen.

How often do you

- listen to your child without thinking about *your* problems?
- listen without walking across the room, washing dishes, paying bills, or skimming the paper?
- listen to your child without interrupting?

How often do you listen without arguing, commenting, disap-
proving, giving advice, or one-upping? ("You think you've got
a problem—guess what happened to me?")

How often do you listen while sitting straight across from your
child, making eye contact, and nodding your head or smiling to
show approval?

If you could critique yourself as a listener, here's what you
might find:

You try to listen. Really, you do. But you rarely follow through.

Around three o'clock you asked Jack how his day was. Then, before he could answer, you told him how your day was.

About three twenty, he started telling you about school, and you started listening, but then you got up to get something from the refrigerator. When you got back, he had left the room.

At seven o'clock, you were doing great, listening to Christine talk about her math class. Then you looked at your watch, saw it was time for the news, and turned on the TV. (You could have used the VCR!) By the time the news was over, Christine was in her room.

TV programmers know that most people can pay attention for ten minutes—that's why commercials are usually ten minutes apart. So we know you can listen to Cosby's kids for ten minutes. . . . But how about your own?

When your child comes home from school tomorrow, sit down across from him and ask him how his day was. (How many times have you asked that question—and then not listened to the answer?) This time, listen. Hold the conversation in a place where your child is comfortable, and avoid interruptions. (You may have to tell your family that "Listening Time" is important.)

To help the conversation along, you can say:

"Really."
"That's great."
"Terrific."
"Tell me more about that."
"That's interesting."
"I love hearing about this."

Or ask:

■ How did you feel about that?
■ What happened next?

- What did she say?
- How did you react?

But don't ask:

- Didn't you feel awful after she did that? (Second-guessing)
- What did I tell you about that yesterday? (Scolding)
- What's the rule on that? (Interrogating)
- You won't make that mistake again, will you? (Advice-giving)

Try to listen for ten minutes at a time. If ten minutes is impossible, aim for three, or five, or seven (approximately—you don't want to keep looking at your watch) and gradually build up to ten.

When you feel comfortable listening to your child, for ten minutes once a day, go on to step 2.

2. Repeat.

CHILD: I'm really lonely.
YOU: You're really lonely.

CHILD: I'm so mad.
YOU: You're so mad.

Repeating forces you to be a good listener. Even if it sounds silly at first, it isn't. You're showing your child that you hear what she's saying, and that's important.

Gradually you can learn to vary the words a little bit to *reflect* rather than simply repeat:

CHILD: I'm so mad.
YOU: You seem really angry about this.

Don't worry: your child won't call you a copycat. If anything, he will enjoy conversing with you more than ever. Because you'll be showing him that you've been listening, that his ideas make sense to you—and that they're even worth repeating.

Some parents have a hard time repeating without "editorializing":

CHILD: I'm angry because the toy broke.
PARENT: You're unhappy because you smashed your new toy.

You may be altering what your child is saying to get him to do what you want him to do.

Keep trying until accurately reflecting what your child is saying comes easily to you. When you are able to accurately reflect what your child says—when "reflecting" has become a habit—go on to step 3.

3. Say you understand.

CHILD: I'm really scared.
YOU: I can understand how scared you are.

You don't have to agree with what he's saying; all you have to do is *understand* it.

CHILD: I'm exhausted from working so hard.

■ Even if she didn't work hard; even if you want her to do more next time; even if you think she's lazy: now isn't the time to say that (not if you care about her self-image).

The "correct" response:

YOU: I understand how exhausted you can get from working.

CHILD: I'm so upset.

- Even if you wouldn't have gotten so upset: don't tell him that—this isn't about what *you* think.

The "correct" response:

YOU: I can appreciate how upset you are about that.

CHILD: Joni doesn't like me anymore, and I hate her.

- Even if you think your child could have been a better friend to Joni; even if you never liked Joni in the first place: save it. The point is to validate your child's feelings.

The "correct" response:

YOU: I can understand how upset you are about her not liking you, and I can see how that might make you hate her.

If you need to know more about what's upsetting your child before you can empathize, ask:

CHILD: I'm so angry about my spelling class.
YOU: What bothered you about it?
CHILD: The teacher said I didn't answer the question she asked, but I did.
YOU: I can understand how upset you are about feeling misunderstood.

CHILD: I'm really mad at Janice.
YOU: What are you upset about?
CHILD: Janice said she didn't want to be my friend anymore.
YOU: What else did she say?
CHILD: She said I'm a bad friend.
YOU: I can see how that would make you angry.

When you are comfortable telling your child you can understand her feelings, go on to step 4.

4. Put it all together.

The most advanced form of empathy is to listen carefully, then paraphrase and summarize what your child has said, indicating a deep level of understanding of his feelings.

Example One:

CHILD: I'm really tired.
YOU: I can understand that you're exhausted after such a difficult day.

Don't put words in his mouth. That can backfire:

YOU: I bet you want to go to bed right away.
CHILD: No, I don't feel like sleeping yet.

Don't one-up:

YOU: You think you're exhausted. How do you think I feel?
CHILD: I don't care how you feel.

Don't scold or try to solve the problem:

YOU: If you went to bed earlier, you wouldn't be so tired after an easy day at school.
CHILD: Well, you may think it was easy!

Example Two:

CHILD: I'm so upset.
YOU: What happened really bothered you. I can see how sad you are. I'm sorry it's so painful.

Don't project your own feelings:

YOU: I bet you want to talk about it. I know I would.
CHILD: No, I just want to sit alone and think.

Example Three:

CHILD: I don't feel like eating anything.
YOU: I can understand that; you're just not hungry.

Don't discount his feelings or tell him he shouldn't have them:

YOU: Oh, you're probably not really full; just wait a few minutes and you'll be able to eat.
CHILD: No, I won't.

Example Four:

CHILD: Martha doesn't like me anymore, and I hate her.
YOU: You're feeling miserable at being deserted by your best friend, and I can understand that. It feels bad to lose a friend. I'm sorry. Let me know if I can do anything to help.

Don't try to solve the problem—not now.

YOU: If you call Martha now, I'm sure she'll want to talk to you.
CHILD: No, she won't. And I wouldn't call her anyway.

Don't give advice yet:

YOU: If you hadn't called your friends names, maybe they wouldn't be so annoyed at you. Try being nicer to your friends next time.
CHILD: I was nice.

Giving advice at this point may embroil you in a disagreement; it certainly won't convey empathy or strengthen your child's self-esteem. Save advice for later, and when you give it, give it lovingly.

YOU: Let's talk about what you can do to be a better friend. [The message is, "You're already a good friend, and you're also a competent enough person to do even better."]

What about discipline?

Giving empathy is *not* the same thing as being permissive.

You can enhance your child's self-image and still be firm. If you want to disagree with what your child is doing, or enforce a rule, or make a point—give empathy first. Once you've let your child know his feelings are understood and accepted, *move to a firm and simple statement of the rule.*

CHILD: I am so angry I am going to miss the show at ten o'clock.
YOU: I understand how you feel. It's upsetting to miss a show you like. [Empathy] But your bedtime is nine o'clock. [Rule]

If your child continues to object

■ give empathy first
■ then replay the rule.

CHILD: Everybody's staying up tonight to watch the show, except me.
YOU: I know it feels terrible to be left out. [Empathy] But you know your bedtime on school nights is nine o'clock. [Replay]
CHILD: You're the strictest parent in town. Everyone else's parents are letting them stay up.

YOU: I know it isn't always fun to have to stick to rules. [Empathy] But we have to stick to your bedtime, which is nine o'clock. [Replay]

In giving empathy before replaying the rule, you are telling your child that you understand and respect his feelings, even when you can't give him what he wants.

JULIE, fourteen: I'm dying to go out with Mark. He's sixteen and just got his license, and he wants to come pick me up in his car.

PARENT: I know how much you want to go out with Mark. He's very special to you. [Empathy] But you can't go out with a boy in a car until you're sixteen. [Rule]

JULIE: But all my friends are allowed to do it now.

PARENT: It must feel terrible to be left out. [Empathy] But you're only fourteen. That's too young for you to go out with a boy in a car. [Replay]

JULIE: But he'll never want to see me again.

PARENT: I can see you're upset, and I'm sorry. [Empathy] But you can't go out on a car date until you're older. [Replay]

RON, ten: I want to swim out to the sailboat in the middle of the lake. I can hardly wait to try it.

PARENT: I know that looks exciting, and you're anxious to see the sailboat. [Empathy] But we agreed you can't go past the ropes until the lifeguard says you're a strong enough swimmer. [Rule]

RON: If you were a nicer mother, you would let me do it.

PARENT: I can understand that it's frustrating to have to wait, and that you don't think I'm being very nice. [Empathy] But we agreed to wait until you have the lifeguard's permission. [Replay]

WENDY, eleven: I want to stay on the phone for a while longer; it's important.

PARENT: I know how much talking to Karen means to you. [Empathy] But you've gone past your hour limit. It's time to get off. [Rule]

WENDY: Karen is allowed to talk until bedtime.

PARENT: I know you wish you could stay on longer. It must seem unfair to you that Karen's family has different rules. [Empathy] But you have a limit—one hour. So now it's time for you to get off. [Replay]

By giving empathy before imposing the rule, you can discipline your child while still enjoying the advantages of being an empathetic parent.

SUMMARY

1. Listen.

Try to listen to your child for ten minutes at least once a day. (You may need to start at three minutes and work up.)

2. Repeat.

Learn to repeat what your child has said. (Child: I'm really disappointed. Parent: You're really disappointed.)

Gradually begin to alter the words—but not the meaning—of what your child is saying. (Child: I'm really disappointed. Parent: You're sorry things didn't work out the way you wanted.)

3. Say you understand.

Let your child know you understand his feelings. You don't have to agree with his feelings to say you understand them. (Child: I'm really disappointed. Parent: I can understand how disappointing that would be.)

If you want to know more about your child's feelings, ask.

Don't be judgmental or try to give advice (not now).

4. Put it all together.

Listen carefully, paraphrase or summarize what your child has said, and indicate a sincere understanding of his feelings. (Child: I'm really disappointed. Parent: I can understand how sad you are that things didn't work out.)

If you need to discipline your child: First: Acknowledge and accept your child's feelings. Then: State the rule you want to enforce. (Parent: I understand that you're upset about being left out. [Empathy] But you can't go out because you haven't finished your homework. [Rule])

If your child keeps arguing, give empathy first, then replay the rule. (Parent: You feel left out, and I understand that you're upset about that. [Empathy] But you're not allowed to go out with your friends until you finish your homework. [Replay])

5

▰▰▰▰▰▰▰▰▰▰▰▰▰▰▰▰▰▰▰▰▰▰▰▰▰▰▰▰▰▰▰▰▰▰▰

THE ART OF
ACCEPTING A COMPLIMENT

ARTHUR'S STORY

By the time he was eight, Arthur could reel off a list of things he didn't like about himself: he was too short, he was too dumb, he was too klutzy.

Criticisms made sense to Arthur, and he accepted them. But compliments didn't fit his view of himself, so he dismissed them.

- Tell him he was handsome, and he'd disagree.
- Tell him he was doing well in school, and he would tell you his teachers were easy graders.
- Tell him he was becoming a good athlete, and he'd say, "Yeah, but not good enough."

It wasn't hard to figure out where Arthur had learned this behavior. His parents, I discovered, were no better at accepting compliments than he was.

Arthur's mother

As a child, her parents had told her that she wasn't pretty, that she couldn't read well, that she wasn't well-coordinated—and the idea stuck.

That was obvious from the way she handled compliments.

- Tell her she looked great in her new dress, and she assumed you were just being sympathetic. "I know I look terrible, but thanks."
- Tell her she was a wonderful mother, and she would disagree. "You don't know. You only think I'm a good mother."
- Praise her for spending hours preparing an elaborate meal, and she would *hear* an insult. "Yeah, a really good cook could have put this meal together in an hour."

Arthur's father

In Arthur's father's family, there was no greater sin than having a "swelled head." From an early age, his parents taught him that it was "conceited" to say—or even think—good things about himself. As a result, even the smallest compliment made him self-conscious.

- Tell him he had done a great job on a report, and he would look down at the floor, shrug, and say, "Well, I got the idea from Ed."
- Notice his handsome new suit, and he would look down at the floor, shrug, and say, "Oh, yeah, I know I'm not much of a dresser, but it was on sale."
- Tell him he was a good friend who had helped during a crisis, and he would look down at the floor, shrug, and say,

"I didn't do anything any person wouldn't have done in the same situation."

Despite all that looking down at the floor, Arthur's father saw that his son had a problem: he was failing to develop a positive self-image. Arthur seemed unhappy, short on self-confidence, and unaware that many people really liked him. He said bad things about himself, and he seemed reluctant to try new things.

Arthur's father knew firsthand what it was like to suffer from a low self-image, and he didn't want his son to experience the same pain.

When I met Arthur's parents at a seminar I was giving, they told me about their son, and they asked me what they could do to help him. I suggested that they compliment Arthur at least four times a day (chapter 2), and I showed them how to do that. They agreed to try.

Two weeks later, they told me they had begun praising their son regularly, just as I'd suggested. But, they said, Arthur didn't seem any more sure of himself than before. Why, they asked, wasn't their praise helping?

I asked how Arthur had reacted to their compliments. They told me.

- He shrugged.
- He ignored them.
- He argued with them.
- He gave someone else the credit.

Here are two conversations Arthur's parents remembered:

MOM: Your room is so much neater; we're proud.
ARTHUR: It looks the same to me.

DAD: Your test score is so much higher than last time. Great.

ARTHUR: Yeah, well, Jenny helped me study.

I told Arthur's parents that their compliments were useless unless Arthur "let them in." And I knew he wouldn't be able to do that as long as his parents were "modeling" the wrong behavior.

When I told Arthur's father how great it was that he was making a special effort to call Arthur on the phone every afternoon and compliment him, he answered, "Oh, it's no big deal. I have to call home anyway."

What Arthur's father should have said is, "Thank you. I really have been making an effort, and I'm glad you noticed."

When I told Arthur's mother how impressed I was that she had found time to give Arthur four compliments a day, with a full-time job to think about, she answered, "Yeah, but I should be doing more. If I were a better mother, Arthur wouldn't be having problems."

What Arthur's mother should have said is, "Yes, it's taken a lot of effort, and I'm proud."

Before Arthur's parents could teach their son how to accept a compliment the right way, I had to teach *them*.

I complimented Arthur's parents, and I asked them to say

"Thank you for noticing."

"I'm glad you like it."

"I'm pleased you think so."

I taught them how to use the right tone of voice when accepting a compliment—"Try to sound warm, accepting, not combative or sarcastic."

I taught them the right body language for accepting a compliment—"Stand or sit up straight, with your heart held high, and make eye contact with the person you're thanking."

"When you accept a compliment," I said, "I want you to *sound* and *look* like you mean it."

To help them practice the techniques, I gave them "easy" compliments—ones they felt comfortable accepting ("That's a nice new dress you have on today."), and I worked with them on their responses.

By our third session, I was giving them "harder" compliments ("You're a very attractive woman." "You've accomplished so much with your life."), and they were accepting them correctly. Now they were ready to share what they had learned with Arthur. I asked them to continue complimenting him at least four times a day, and to teach him the right words, the right tone of voice, and the right body language for responding. Most important, I asked them to continue "modeling" the correct behavior whenever anyone complimented one of them.

Two weeks later, they reported back to me again. They told me they were still complimenting Arthur regularly. If he downgraded the compliment, they gave him empathy—"We know how hard it is to do this." Then they suggested a better way of responding, and they complimented him again. Most of the time he was able to get the words, the tone of voice, and even the body language right. Arthur's parents were thrilled. For the first time, he was accepting the praise they gave him. And his self-image seemed to be improving. (How did they know that? He reported positives about himself. He talked about his achievements instead of his failures. And he was excited, rather than scared, to try new things.)

I told Arthur's mother how glad I was that she had helped Arthur so much. She said, "Thank you. I'm so glad I've been able to help him."

I told Arthur's father how great it was that he was helping to improve Arthur's self-image. He said, "Thank you. It's nice of you to recognize how hard we've been trying."

I knew Arthur was in good hands.

▀▀▀

Most of us have no idea how to accept a compliment correctly. We're afraid that if we agree with the person who complimented us, we'll sound conceited. Sometimes, just thinking about the compliment can make us feel self-conscious. So we look down at the floor. We turn around. We blush or give a "Who, me?" look. We don't say thank you. Or if we do, we whisper it. Or mumble. We give credit to everyone but ourselves. And we question the complimenter's motives ("Why would he be saying that about me? He must want something.") or sanity ("She's crazy if she thinks that.").

Criticism, which reinforces what we believe about ourselves, is easy for us to accept. In fact, it sometimes stays with us for days, weeks—even years. But praise goes "in one ear and out the other." We discount it, we ignore it, we disown it.

Some of us feel starved for praise. *Ironically, we may be getting all the praise we need.* But we don't hear it. We dismiss it or shrug it off—before it can have a positive effect on our self-image.

Praise can only make your child feel better about herself if she learns to accept it. The rules for doing that are pretty simple. (You can teach them to your child in a couple of days.) But first you'll have to learn them yourself, and begin using them in front of your child. When it comes to accepting praise, what you *do* may affect your child even more than what you tell him.

Learning to accept compliments will have a dramatic impact on your child's self-image. One day he will just be following the rules mechanically; the next day he'll be following them naturally, and feeling better about himself as a person.

Rules for accepting compliments

Don't ignore the complimenter.
Don't downgrade the compliment.
Don't question the motives of the complimenter.
Don't mock the compliment.
Don't question the intelligence of the complimenter.
Don't question the sanity of the complimenter.
Don't give the credit to someone else.
Don't shrug.
Don't look down at the floor.
Don't turn around.
Don't walk away.
Don't look pained.
Don't look confused.
Don't say, "Who, me?"
Don't whisper.
Don't mumble.
Don't say, "You're kidding."
Don't giggle.
Don't turn around.
Don't run for cover.
Don't say, "But it was an accident."
Don't say, "But I could have done better."
Don't say, "But it's no big deal."
Don't say, "Yes, but . . ."
Don't say, "Maybe, but . . ."
Don't say, "Okay, but . . ."

Do acknowledge the compliment.

Do thank the complimenter.

Do rephrase the compliment as part of your thank you.

Example:

COMPLIMENTER: Your hair looks great.

YOU: Thank you for saying that you like my hair. I like this style too.

(A simple "thank you" is a good start. But "thank you" can be a throwaway, a phrase you barely remember saying. By including the compliment in your response, you're taking the time to acknowledge that you've really heard it.)

- Make eye contact with the complimenter.
- Speak loudly and clearly.
- Sit or stand up straight (with heart held high).
- Return the compliment. ("It was so thoughtful of you to notice.")

Practice the rules.

Find someone to practice with—your "partner" can be your spouse, a friend, or one of *your* parents.

Take turns giving each other compliments.

If at first you can't think of compliments to give, choose some from this list:

- That outfit is really flattering on you.
- It was so thoughtful of you to come and see me.
- You're such a great parent for putting time into these self-esteem exercises.
- You're a very warm person—I always feel safe with you.

- You're so much fun to be with.
- You look very handsome.
- Since you bought that self-esteem book, you've been so much more upbeat.

If your partner doesn't accept your compliment "correctly," give the same compliment again, with appropriate advice.

HUSBAND: You're looking very attractive today.

WIFE: Thanks, but not attractive enough.

HUSBAND: I think you can accept the compliment more gracefully than that. Just say "Thank you." If you're nervous, try closing your eyes and thinking of a pleasant scene, like the ocean, before you accept the compliment. Okay. You're looking very attractive today.

WIFE. (*Mumbling*) I look okay, I suppose.

HUSBAND: Let's try it again. This time, leave out "I suppose." Here goes. You're looking very attractive today.

WIFE: (*Softly*) Yes, I have lost weight, and I'm feeling good. Thank you for noticing.

HUSBAND: That was great. But now try saying it a little more convincingly. This time, look me in the eye. Okay, here goes. You're looking very attractive today.

WIFE: (*Loudly and confidently*) Well, I do feel terrific. Thank you so much for noticing.

Keep practicing, even after it's easy for you to say the right words. Practice until accepting compliments gracefully is a habit you can't break.

Transfer your new skill to real-life situations. Keep track of how you accept the compliments you get from friends, coworkers, your boss, your husband or wife, your parents, your children. If, for at least a week, you have followed most of the rules most of the time (nobody's perfect), you're ready to start teaching your child what you've learned.

Make teaching the rules a game.

For a four-year-old: I'm going to say something I like about you, and let's see what you say back to me. This should be fun.

For a ten-year-old: I'm going to show you a new way to accept compliments, which will help you feel good about yourself. Let's make it a game.

You may find it helps to use small rewards: coins, candies, or points (which can add up to a reward): "Every time you give me the right answer, I'll give you a point. When you have twenty points, I'll take you to the zoo."

Use role reversal.

YOU: Okay, I'll be you, and you be Aunt Sophie. Tell me how much you like my new dress. Go ahead.

CHILD: I like your new dress.

YOU (playing the role of your child): Thank you. I'm so happy you noticed.

Use behavior rehearsal.

Ask your child to let you know how he responds to compliments from others (teachers, grandparents, friends). If he's doing the appropriate things, congratulate him. If not, you may want to rehearse his responses. ("Okay, I'll be Mrs. Mercer. I'll compliment you, and you respond . . .")

Use prompts and cues.

A prompt is a way of letting the other person know exactly what to say.

YOU: I think you're doing wonderfully at the piano. Now say, "Thanks. I'm glad you think so."

A cue is simply a reminder to respond.

YOU: You look so cute with your new haircut. Now it's time for you to accept the compliment.

Don't expect a perfect response right at the beginning.

- The first time you give your child a compliment, she may say nothing. That's okay; if she doesn't downgrade or dismiss it, she's already taken an important step.
- The next time it's enough for her to mumble, "Thank you."
- The next time, she should try to say "Thank you" with a stronger voice.
- The next time she can add a few words. "Thank you for noticing."
- Then she can try to add eye contact.
- Then she can stand or sit up straight, with her heart held high.
- Next she can use the right tone of voice.
- Finally, she can rephrase the compliment as part of her thank you. "Thanks, Mom, for noticing how hard I worked on my homework."

Start off giving your child compliments that are easy for her to accept ("The colors on your painting are so bright."). Gradually work your way up to broader, more personal compliments ("You're a wonderful daughter."), which she may find harder to acknowledge.

Keep at it.

When your child downgrades a compliment, give him the same compliment again, adding prompts or cues as necessary. If you have to, keep repeating the same compliment, over and over, until he accepts it correctly.

"Okay, I'm going to give you the compliment again. This time, when I tell you I like your shirt, try to look me in the eye and say 'Thank you.' "

Or, if your child feels anxious, suggest that he close his eyes and think about a relaxing scene before responding.

Do four a day.

By now, you should be trying to compliment your child at least four times a day (see chapter 2). Each time you compliment your child, pay attention to his response. (Think of each compliment you give your child as the occasion for an impromptu practice session.)

Use positive reinforcement.

After your child accepts a compliment correctly, tell her you're glad. Tell her it's great that she's making such an effort. Tell her you're thrilled that she's made so much progress.

YOU: I really like the way you cleaned your room.
CHILD: Thanks, Mom, for telling me that you noticed.
YOU: I'm so glad you are accepting compliments so well now.

Have your child keep a list.

If your child says, "But no one compliments me," you may want to show him that that isn't true—that he may not be aware of all the compliments he's getting. Ask him to keep a list of all the nice things people say to him. Have him include statements like, "Our time together is always too short," which is as much a compliment as "You're so good-looking." Hang each day's (or each week's) list in a place where he can see it.

Josh, ten, gets all A's but says it's luck. He's about to start middle school, and he's unsure about his ability to get good grades there.

FATHER: You did a great job on your English paper.

JOSH: Oh, the teacher was in a good mood today.

FATHER: Now try to accept the compliment by saying "Thank you." You did really nicely on your English paper.

JOSH: *(With eye contact)* Thanks, Dad.

FATHER: Great, that was a lot better.

Trudy, five, is hesitant about going to school, and when she gets there, she's shy around her classmates.

TEACHER: That was a great try.

TRUDY: Yeah, but I didn't get it right.

TEACHER: *(Repeating)* This time don't downgrade the compliment. Say, "Thank you. I'm really glad you said that." Okay, I'm going to compliment you again. That was a great try, Trudy.

TRUDY: Thank you. I'm really glad you said that.

TEACHER: Terrific.

Keith, eight, gets along well with other kids but has a learning disability that frustrates him in class.

MOTHER: I liked how well you read that to me.

KEITH: Well, it was a really easy story.

MOTHER: Now try to accept the compliment without putting yourself down. Don't put in the part about it being an easy story. Try to just say thank you. Okay, I liked how well you read that to me.

KEITH: Thanks, I'm glad you liked it.

MOTHER: Great.

Margaret, eight, often throws temper tantrums.

FATHER: It was nice of you to write down the telephone message from Mark.

(*Margaret shrugs*)

FATHER: Try to accept the compliment with a "thank you" this time. It was nice of you to write down the telephone message from Mark.

MARGARET: It was no big deal.

FATHER: Let's try again. See if you can accept the compliment without dismissing it. It was nice of you to write down the telephone message from Mark.

MARGARET: Thank you for telling me.

FATHER: Very good. You said the right thing, but now look me directly in the eyes as you say it. It was nice of you to write down the telephone message from Mark.

MARGARET: (*With eye contact*) Thank you for telling me.

FATHER: That's it!

SUMMARY

Plan of action:

1. Learn the rules for accepting compliments.
2. Practice the rules with a partner.
3. Once the rules are second nature to you, begin teaching them to your child.
4. Practice regularly. Try to give your child at least four compliments a day, and work on his response each time.

Rules for accepting compliments:

- Don't downgrade or ignore the compliment.
- Don't sneer, giggle nervously, or question the complimenter's motives.
- Thank the complimenter. Simply saying "Thank you" is okay. But try to say more: "Thank you for noticing that I'm wearing a new dress."
- Don't look down; look straight ahead, making eye contact with the complimenter.
- Don't whisper or mumble; acknowledge the compliment clearly.

How to teach your child:

- Use prompts. ("Now you say . . .")
- Use cues. ("Okay, go ahead and accept the compliment.")
- Use role reversal ("I'll be you and you be me.") and behavior rehearsal ("I'll be Mrs. Kaplan . . . ").
- Offer rewards (prizes or points).
- Use positive reinforcement (when your child accepts a compliment correctly, praise her).

- Start with compliments that are easy for your child to accept. ("I love the color of your dress.") Gradually work your way up to global ones. ("You're a wonderful person.")
- Have your child keep a list of compliments she receives (there may be more of them than she realizes).

6

▀▀▀

THE EMOTIONAL SHRUG: DEALING WITH CRITICISM

RICHARD'S STORY

During my first conversation with Richard's parents, they told me that they criticized their son a lot. They weren't proud of that, exactly. But they figured it was necessary. After all, they said, there were a lot of things to criticize about him.

At nine, according to his parents, Richard should have been a terrific athlete, an ambitious student, and a popular all-around guy. But he wasn't any of those things. He was, his parents told me, an undistinguished athlete, a mediocre student, and a loner who spent nights and weekends by himself watching TV.

When his parents tried to talk to him about his problems, they said, they were unable to get him to respond. He either argued with them or refused to talk at all. Getting him to change his ways seemed hopeless.

At my first meeting with Richard and his parents, I asked each of them to tell me more about their family. Richard said nothing, but his parents began reeling off a list of complaints:

- Richard didn't have enough friends.
- Richard wasn't trying hard enough in school.
- Richard didn't clean his room.
- Richard spent too much time in front of the TV.

I asked Richard's parents if they would be willing to learn to criticize Richard less often.

FATHER: Well, we don't like criticizing him. But all the things we've said are true, and they're all important for Richard to hear. We want him to improve.
ME: What if I could show you how to accomplish more while criticizing less?
FATHER: Well, that would be terrific.

Then I asked Richard how his parents' criticisms made him feel. He said, "Well, I guess they're right to say those things. I feel like a failure. I'm not the kind of kid they wanted."

I asked Richard's mother why they criticized their son.

MOTHER: All we want to do is get him to achieve more, so he can have a better life.
ME: Do you mean to hurt him?
MOTHER: No, of course not.
ME: Do you think you have been hurting him?
MOTHER: I guess so, but I don't know what to do about it.

I asked Richard if his parents' criticisms hurt him.

RICHARD: I guess so. I mean, I'm trying to be a good son, but they aren't happy.

Then I asked Richard The Question—"Tell me something you like about yourself" (chapter 3)—and, though I encouraged him to answer, he was silent. His parents seemed surprised.

When I asked Richard what he *didn't* like about himself, he had no trouble answering; indeed, his list sounded almost exactly like his father's:

- I don't have enough friends.
- I'm not trying hard enough in school.
- I never clean my room.

Richard's parents may have thought their son wasn't paying attention when they criticized him, but obviously he was. In fact, he probably remembered too much. His parents' criticisms were damaging his self-esteem. When I mentioned that to them, they nodded.

With Richard out of the room, I told his parents that it's natural for parents to criticize their children, and I empathized with them. ("I understand that you want your son to be successful.") But I explained that their criticism was damaging his self-esteem—and that's all it was doing.

"I can see that now," said Richard's mother.

I suggested that they try another approach. I asked them to try to reduce the number of times they criticized their son, and I showed them how to do that (chapter 2). They said they would try, and I praised them for making an effort.

I told them I would like to meet with Richard privately to teach him a new way to respond to criticism. Some criticism, from them and others, is inevitable, I said, and I wanted Richard to be able to accept that criticism without letting it hurt his self-esteem. After I had taught Richard my way of handling criticism, I said, I would invite his parents back to help him practice it in real-life situations.

During our first session together, I told Richard that I was going to teach him how to learn from criticism, but not let it destroy him; to hear it, accept it or reject it, then not be bothered by it. Soon, I said, criticism wouldn't loom over him threateningly; it would just roll off him. He seemed eager to begin.

But first, I said, I needed to know more about him. I asked him to imagine people criticizing him, and to tell me what they said. Every few minutes, I gave Richard a break, during which I urged him to think about something positive (getting one hundred on a test, swimming in a mountain lake, spending a whole day at the movies). In that way, Richard was able to spend an hour talking about criticism without becoming noticeably anxious.

Here are some of the criticisms Richard remembered:

A FRIEND: You're a bad baseball player.

A BOY IN HIS GYM CLASS: We don't want you on our team. You never score.

ANOTHER BOY IN HIS GYM CLASS: You're a sore loser.

A TEACHER: Richard, you don't speak in class enough.

HIS MOTHER: You're not like other kids. You never go out and play.

HIS FATHER: You dropped the ball again!

HIS FATHER: You're spending too much time watching TV.

HIS FATHER: Your grades are a major disappointment.

HIS FATHER: You'll never make friends if you keep playing that way.

A GIRL IN HIS CLASS: I don't think anybody in this class really likes you.

I praised Richard for helping ("I'm sure it isn't fun to talk about those things, but it's important for me to know about them."). Then I told him that I needed to find out which criticisms hurt him a lot, and which only a little. In other words, I needed to form a criticism hierarchy.

Making Richard's hierarchy

I asked Richard to tell me how much each criticism hurt him, on a scale of one (very little) to ten (a lot). If he couldn't think of a number, I asked him to show me with his hand—holding it way up high for something that hurt a lot, and down low for something that only hurt a little. Gradually we formed this "criticism hierarchy."

RICHARD'S HIERARCHY

From least to most hurtful:

1. A teacher tells him, "You don't speak in class enough."
2. His father says, "Richard, you dropped the ball again."
3. His father says, "Your grades are a major disappointment."
4. His father says, "You're spending too much time watching TV."
5. His mother says, "You're not like other kids. You never go out and play."
6. A friend says, "You're a bad baseball player."
7. A boy in his gym class says, "You're a sore loser."
8. Another boy in his gym class says, "We don't want you on our team. You never score."
9. His father says, "You'll never make friends if you keep playing that way."
10. A girl in his class says, "I don't think anybody in this class really likes you."

Deserved criticism: The emotional shrug

With his hierarchy to guide me, I was ready to begin teaching Richard how to deal with *deserved* criticism. My goal, I said, was

to teach him to greet deserved criticism with an emotional shrug
—an internal reaction that says, "I hear you, but I'm not letting
it get to me. Even if what you're saying is true, it isn't the end
of the world." I told him I would help him practice the shrug,
until it became his automatic reaction to deserved criticism.

I told Richard that I was going to pretend to be his father, and
I was going to tell him, "Richard, you dropped the ball again."
I asked him to "act out" his normal reaction to that kind of
criticism.

ME: You dropped the ball again.
RICHARD: I know. I'm not good at sports.
ME: Richard, you're putting yourself down. It sounds like your
father's criticism hurt you. Try giving me the criticism, and let's
see if I can handle it differently. Okay, go ahead.
RICHARD: You dropped the ball again.
ME: You're right, I did drop the ball.
RICHARD: You mean I should admit I dropped it, just like that?
ME: Sure. You did drop it. But it's no big deal. You're still a
worthwhile person. And you want that to come across.
RICHARD: Okay, I'm ready to try it.
ME: Okay. I'll give you the criticism this time. You dropped the
ball again.
RICHARD: I forgot. What am I supposed to do?
ME: Look and sound like you're in control. Don't look hurt if you
can help it. Try saying, "You're right. I dropped the ball again."
RICHARD: Okay.
ME: You dropped the ball again.
RICHARD: You're right. I dropped the ball again.
ME: Great. You said that just right. But you still looked hurt. Try
it again, and this time try to seem unfazed. Sit up straight—with
your heart held high—and look right at me. Okay, let's try it.
You dropped the ball again.

RICHARD: You're right. I dropped the ball again.

ME: Great. You did that just right. You said the right things, and you looked in control. Now you know the right way to handle deserved criticism. All we need to do is practice.

During the next few weeks, we practiced Richard's response to deserved criticism, using his hierarchy as a guide.

ME: Okay, I'm going to criticize you again. I'm going to pretend I'm that big boy who's always criticizing you in school. Okay?

RICHARD: Okay.

ME: Richard, we don't want you on our team. You never score.

RICHARD: (Defiantly) Oh, yeah! Well, you're ugly and stupid.

ME: Richard, you overreacted, and you got nasty. Anybody watching would have known my criticism really hurt you.

RICHARD: Yeah, it did.

ME: Okay, that's understandable. And I'm glad you're being so honest. But I think my way of responding to criticism will let you feel better about yourself inside. Do you think you can do the emotional shrug next time?

RICHARD: I'll try.

ME: Good. And while you're shrugging, I want you say, "You're absolutely right, I don't score very often." I want you to sound confident and in control.

RICHARD: Okay.

ME: Here goes. Richard, we don't want you on our team. You never score.

RICHARD: You're right. I don't score very often.

ME: Very good. You even looked confident when you said that. How did you feel?

RICHARD: I felt confident, like I didn't have to explain myself, or fight back. I just felt good.

ME: Great. You see, you can't necessarily be the best baseball player in your class, but you can learn not to let that upset you.

RICHARD: You're right. That time it didn't.

Undeserved criticism: The respectful BUT

I asked Richard to think about how he dealt with *undeserved* criticism.

ME: Richard, I'm going to give you some inaccurate criticism, and I'd like you to show me how you react.

RICHARD: Okay.

ME: Richard, I'm really mad at you. You're always late for our appointments.

RICHARD: You're crazy.

ME: Okay, but how do you think that's going to make me feel?

RICHARD: It'll probably make you angry.

ME: Right, I'll probably start arguing with you. Instead, I want you to "empathize" with me. That means you should show me that you understand how I feel, even if you don't agree with it.

RICHARD: How do I do that?

ME: Say something like, "I understand how you can feel that way." That doesn't mean you agree; you're just acknowledging my feelings. Okay, I'll criticize you again. You're always late for our appointments.

RICHARD: Okay. I understand how you could feel that way.

ME: Is there anything else you want to say?

RICHARD: I've been on time the last three weeks.

ME: Great. By saying that, you stood up for yourself. You stated your position. But you didn't get angry or criticize back. You seemed competent, in control. Now, what would you do if I kept arguing?

RICHARD: I don't know.

ME: Make your point over and over. Don't get mad; just hold your ground.

RICHARD: Okay.

ME: Let's try it. I'm still mad at you, because you're always late.

RICHARD: You think I've been late, but I've been on time for the last three weeks.

ME: Richard, I'm going to keep criticizing you. I'm so angry. You're always late. Now, do it again.

RICHARD: I know you're angry. But I've been on time for the last three weeks.

ME: You're an irresponsible person.

RICHARD: You may feel that way, but I've been on time for the last three weeks.

ME: Why do you keep repeating yourself?

RICHARD: Because I've been on time for the last three weeks.

ME: Great. You stuck to your guns. You were in control. That was really terrific, Richard. Just keep saying it as many times as you have to.

(A minute later)

ME: Let's try it again. I'll give you more undeserved criticism. Richard, you're a really lazy kid.

RICHARD: But I'm not lazy.

ME: Yes, you are.

RICHARD: No, I'm not.

ME: Okay, we're having a fight. Can you see that this isn't going to get us anywhere?

RICHARD: Yes.

ME: So let's try doing it my way. Acknowledge that I criticized you while still holding your ground.

RICHARD: Okay.

ME: You're lazy. You're so lazy. Now, say you understand that

I feel that way, but you've been doing four hours of homework a night.

RICHARD: I understand that I may seem lazy to you, but I've been doing four hours of homework a night.

ME: Four hours? Hah.

RICHARD: Yes. I know you think I'm lazy, but I've been doing four hours of homework a night.

ME: I guess you're not lazy. . . . You see, I even admitted I was wrong—something I probably wouldn't have done if you had argued back. How did it feel to react the way you did?

RICHARD: I felt in control.

ME: Terrific. You seemed really competent in the face of all my unfair criticism.

For the next two weeks, we practiced Richard's reaction to undeserved criticism. Each time I criticized him, Richard empathized with me—then stated his position firmly. No matter how many times I repeated my criticism, he didn't get angry. He just stuck to his guns.

Next I had a talk with Richard's parents. I told them that Richard had learned a new way of dealing with criticism, which I said would enable him to "accept" it without allowing it to hurt his self-esteem. I told them how Richard might behave the next time they criticized him. Instead of punishing him for his assertive responses, which might sound strange to them at first, I asked them to praise Richard for learning an important new skill.

The next week, Richard's parents accompanied him to my office. I asked Richard's parents to criticize him, the way they had done so often in the past. Here's what happened.

ME: *(To Richard's father)* First, try giving him some deserved criticism.

FATHER: Your grades are disappointing. You've gotten lots of B's.

RICHARD: You're right. I did get mostly B's. But I'll try to do better.

ME: *(To Richard)* How did that feel to you?

RICHARD: Well, I heard what my father said, and I'll try to do something about it. It still bothered me, but not as much as it used to

ME: Fine. *(To Richard's father)* How do you feel about what just happened?

FATHER: Well, I'm glad that Richard doesn't seem upset. It sounds like he heard what I said, and he's going to try to do something about it. That's all I want. I never wanted to make him feel bad. If he can hear my criticism without letting it hurt him, and try to do something about it, that's terrific.

MOTHER: I agree.

ME: *(To Richard's mother)* Can you try criticizing Richard? Try telling him something that isn't really accurate, something you might say when you're angry at him.

MOTHER: Richard, you spend too much time alone in your room, watching TV, and you're not getting your homework done because of it.

RICHARD: I understand how you feel. But I'm getting all my homework done before I watch TV.

ME: *(To Richard's mother)* Do you feel like following up?

MOTHER: *(To Richard)* You just watch too much TV. It makes me mad to see you watching TV when you could be doing your homework.

RICHARD: Well, I understand how you feel. I can see that you're unhappy about it. But I don't agree with you. I have been getting all my homework done.

ME: *(To Richard)* How did that make you feel?

RICHARD: Well, I heard what my mother said without letting it hurt me. And I was able to tell her how I felt without getting into an argument. But maybe that's because you were here.

ME: Maybe that's part of it, but you'll learn how to do this without me. *(To Richard's mother)* How did you feel about that discussion?

(Mother is silent)

ME: Did it feel like he was defying you?

MOTHER: Yes, a little.

ME: Richard, do you feel like you were defying your mother?

RICHARD: No, not at all. I heard what she said, and I told her that. But I don't want to let it hurt me.

ME: *(To Richard's mother)* What kind of reaction are you used to getting when you criticize Richard?

MOTHER: Well, he would usually get defensive and look crushed.

ME: In a way, that made you more comfortable, because you could see that your criticism was getting through to him.

MOTHER: Yes.

ME: But it was getting through to him in totally the wrong way. Can you see that?

MOTHER: Yes. But I'd still like him to watch less TV. Isn't there some way for me to tell him that?

ME: Sure there is. You're his mother, and it's your right to tell him how you'd like him to behave. But you can do that without criticizing. By all means tell him what to do, but don't damage his self-esteem in the process.

MOTHER: Okay.

ME: What would you say if you wanted him to watch less TV?

MOTHER: Richard, you're watching much too much TV, and I don't like it. You're in front of the set all day. Starting tomorrow, you're not going to be allowed to watch more than two hours a night.

ME: You've made criticism a part of your instruction to Richard. You're hurting his self-esteem, when what you really want to do

is change his behavior. Why not leave the criticism out of it? Just say, "From now on, I'd like you to limit yourself to two hours of television a night." Period. That way, you haven't hurt his self-esteem. He can just agree to watch less TV, and that's that.
MOTHER: Okay. I'll try that.

During the next few weeks, I asked Richard to keep track of how many criticisms he got and how he handled them. Here are two examples he remembered:

RICHARD'S FATHER: You never catch the ball.
RICHARD: I know you feel that way, but I do catch it sometimes.

A CLASSMATE: You only got a seventy-five on the test.
RICHARD: You're right. I did get a seventy-five.

Naturally I praised Richard for not arguing, not apologizing, and not giving in. He had become a master of the emotional shrug.

By now, Richard didn't seem glum all the time; he seemed more sure of himself, and he could converse intelligently and calmly with his parents—even about his faults. They didn't criticize him nearly as often as they had before, but when they did, Richard's self-image didn't suffer.

No matter what, you're going to criticize your child.

- You've had a hard day at the office, and your child is making too much noise.

- Company's coming, and his room is a mess.
- In an attempt to cook breakfast for the family, he's wasted twenty dollars' worth of groceries.

You don't want to hurt your child. But you're human.

Criticism without pain

Try—when you have to criticize your child—to do it without hurting.

- Instead of "You're the messiest kid I've ever seen," try, "I think it would be better if you cleaned your room more often."

- Instead of, "You're failing math because you're lazy," try, "It seems like if you spent more time on your homework, you could probably pull your grade up."

- Instead of, "You're tone deaf; you'll never be a singer," try, "If you want to sing better, maybe we can get you lessons."

If you've read chapter 1, you're probably giving your child positive reinforcement regularly. Congratulations. Praise can soften the effects of criticism. But unfortunately, all the praise in the world won't stop your child from feeling bad when you criticize him.

Why do you criticize your child?

- To encourage your child to do better ("constructive" criticism)
- To vent emotions

You don't criticize your child to make him feel bad about himself, to make him feel unworthy, to damage his self-image. But that may be exactly what you're doing.

When you say, "You're the messiest child I've ever seen," you may just want your child to clean his room. But what does he hear? "I'm a bad kid. I'm useless. I'm unworthy of love."

When you say, "You're too noisy," you may just be trying to get some peace and quiet. But what does she hear? "I'm a pain in the neck. My mother doesn't like me. Or love me."

You're going to keep criticizing your child, no matter what. You're human. But you can teach your child to accept your criticism without letting it damage his self-esteem.

I'm going to ask you to teach your child to accept criticism with equanimity. Not to apologize, not to be defensive—but to accept it without caving in.

Dealing with deserved criticism

Here's how your child may respond to deserved criticism:

YOU: Your room is a mess again.
CHILD: No, it's not.

YOU: Your room is a mess again.
CHILD: I'm really sorry. But I've just been too busy to clean it.

or

YOU: Your room is a mess again.
CHILD: Stop picking on me. Tommy's room is a mess, and you never complain to him.

Here's how your child *should* be responding to deserved criticism:

YOU: Your room is a mess again.

CHILD: You're right. My room is a mess. I'll clean it up in a few minutes.

At first your child's reaction may sound strange to you. After all, he isn't giving in, or fighting back. It may sound like he's defying you. He isn't. What he's doing is accepting your criticism without sacrificing his self-esteem.

Allow your child to respond this way (even if it seems strange to you at first). Praise him for learning a new, more effective behavior.

Knowing how to deal with criticism effectively can be an important weapon against negative peer pressure, particularly in adolescence.

"Hey, come on, you're stupid not to have a beer. Everyone in school drinks."

If your child can learn to handle that kind of criticism, he will be able to make his own decisions.

Why don't I just stop criticizing my child completely? Wouldn't that be better for his self-image?

Even if you could stop criticizing your child, other people won't. Teachers, grandparents, aunts, uncles, and other children may be pounding your child with criticism.

Indeed, your child will endure criticism throughout his life, unless he refuses to interact with people. As Dr. Joseph Wolpe, a wise and wonderful man, once told me, "If no one criticizes you, you're not doing anything important."

If your child lives his life in order to avoid criticism, he may

be avoiding making an impact; he may be avoiding the contro-
versial and settling for the mediocre.

You can't teach your child to avoid criticism. But you can
teach your child to deal with criticism without letting it hurt him.

Begin my telling him the truth. Tell him that, throughout his
life, he's going to face criticism. And tell him that you want him
to be able to accept that criticism, and even to learn from it—but
that you don't want it to hurt him.

Tell him the work you're going to do on accepting criticism
will be in the form of a game. If you like, offer him prizes ("If
you work with me every day for a week, I'll give you art lessons."
"When you learn this technique, we'll celebrate with a trip to the
circus."). Set aside ten minutes a day for your "criticism project"—for at least two weeks.

Before you can help your child, you're going to have to find
out more about the criticism he already gets. Ask him to tell you
some of the critical things people have said to him. And don't
be shocked if most of the criticisms he remembers came from
you.

Slowly ask your child how bad each of those criticisms feels.
If he's old enough, ask him to rate them on a one-to-ten scale.
Otherwise, have him describe the impact of each criticism in
words ("Is that one really bad? Or just a little hurtful?"). Or
have him indicate how bad each criticism is by moving his hand
up and down (at his waist is a one, at his shoulders is a five, and
way over his head is a ten). Use this information to put together
a hierarchy of criticisms, from least to most hurtful. The hierarchy is a guide that will enable you to teach your child the techniques for handling criticism gradually, without throwing him in
"over his head."

Here is the hierarchy Carl, a seven-year-old, made with his
mother.

CARL'S HIERARCHY

From least to most hurtful:

1. My brother said I wasn't smart.

2. A younger child at school told me I don't dress very nicely.

3. My mother said I didn't do a good job cleaning my room.

4. My teacher told me I wasn't conscientious because I came late to class.

5. My father said I was inconsiderate for monopolizing the phone.

6. Mrs. Thomas said I didn't do a good job writing the book report.

7. The baseball coach said I had to sit out the game because my hitting is bad.

8. Tommy said I didn't look muscular.

9. I overheard Debbie telling her friends that I'm not very nice.

10. Jimmy and Eric said I'm weird because I read so much.

Try some of the deserved criticisms on your child, to see how he reacts.

If he's like most children, he'll be defensive.

YOU: You didn't make your bed again.
CHILD: Well, I slept late, then Jennifer called, and I needed time to feed my fish. I didn't have time to make it.

YOU: You handed in your book report late.
CHILD: Well, I didn't know it was due, and I had so much arithmetic to do over the weekend, and I got a cold. It was hard to work when my nose was running.

There's nothing wrong with responding to criticism with legitimate excuses. But you've probably heard the excuses before;

your child isn't telling you anything important. Instead, he is making himself feel weak. And being defensive is sure to have a negative impact on his self-image. Tell him that it's normal to make mistakes, to do things wrong—and to be criticized. Tell him you're going to show him a new way to accept criticism without letting it damage his self-image.

Role reversal

Play the part of your child:

PARENT: You be your teacher, Mrs. Jeeves, and I'll be you. Tell me that I'm late, and I'll show you a new way to answer. It's called the "emotional shrug."
CHILD: You're late for class again.
PARENT: You're right. I am late, and I'm sorry. You see what I did? I didn't make excuses. I just accepted the criticism, which was deserved, but I didn't let it upset me. In a way, I shrugged inside.
CHILD: Uh-huh.
PARENT: Okay, now give me another one.
CHILD: You didn't make your bed again.
PARENT: You're right. It's not made yet. I'll make it right now.

Behavior rehearsal

Now ask your child to play himself. Criticize him, and then encourage him (with prompts and cues) to try the emotional shrug:

PARENT: You're late. Now remember, don't make excuses. Just say, "You're right. I'm late, and I'm sorry."
CHILD: You're right. I'm late, and I'm sorry.

PARENT: That's really good. Next time, don't look like you're ashamed. Look me in the eye if you can.

CHILD: Okay, I'll try.

PARENT: Here's another one. You didn't make your bed. You never make it without being reminded three times. Now remember, don't argue with me, and don't give excuses. Just agree. Say, "You're right. I forgot to make it, and I'll do it now." And try to look me in the eye.

CHILD: Okay.

PARENT: Okay, I'll criticize you. You didn't make your bed again.

CHILD: Yes, I forgot to make it. You're right, and I'll make it now.

PARENT: Great.

(The next day)

PARENT: Let's practice handling deserved criticism again. I'll criticize you for not feeding the fish when you were supposed to. Agree that you forgot, but don't be defensive. Remember, you're human. Here goes. You didn't feed the fish when you were supposed to.

CHILD: Oh, I forgot. I'm sorry.

PARENT: That's great. You even looked me in the eye when you said that. Now, we'll do it again, and this time I'll be your teacher. You handed in your paper late again. Now, remember, you're human, and it's okay to make mistakes. It's better to hand your papers in on time, but no one is perfect. Just accept that you made a mistake and tell the teacher you're sorry. Okay?

CHILD: Okay.

PARENT: Here goes. Jimmy, you turned your paper in late again.

CHILD: You're right. It was late, and I'm sorry.

PARENT: Great. I'll do another one as your teacher. Jimmy, you forgot to do part of your vocabulary list.

CHILD: Mrs. Owens, you're absolutely right. I totally overlooked that part of the list.

PARENT: Terrific.

(The next day)

PARENT: Let's replay our conversation from Sunday night. I criticized you, and you were very defensive about it.

CHILD: Okay.

PARENT: Remember, your room was a mess, or at least I thought it was. You had spent the day watching a game on TV, trading baseball cards, and talking on the phone. When I criticized the mess, you said you were tired, had a lot of schoolwork, and had a headache.

CHILD: I remember.

PARENT: Well, there are two problems with excuses like that. First, they make you feel weak. Second, they give me a lot of room to argue with you. And neither of us really wants to argue. Remember, as soon as you gave those excuses, Daddy started disagreeing with every one of them.

CHILD: Uh-huh.

PARENT: Well, let's assume that your room really was a mess, that you were supposed to clean it but didn't, and that I criticized you. This time, accept the criticism. You'll feel stronger, and Daddy and I won't come after you with more criticism. Just agree that your room is a mess, and say that you'll do your best to clean it up by bedtime. Let's try.

CHILD: Okay.

PARENT: Jimmy, your room is still a mess, and it's almost bedtime.

CHILD: You're right, it is a mess, and I'll do as much as I can to clean it up before bedtime.

PARENT: Do you feel better than you did on Sunday?

CHILD: Yes. I feel more in control.
PARENT: Great. That's what I was hoping to hear.

Dealing with undeserved criticism

Sometimes your child will receive criticism that is totally un-called for:

- Your child arrives at a babysitting job on time, and his employer tells him he's late.
- Her teacher misplaces her report, then criticizes her for not turning it in.
- You criticize him for not doing enough homework, when, in fact, he was doing it quietly in his room all afternoon.
- She waits her turn to use the swing on the playground, but another child accuses her of cutting in.

In these situations, your child's natural tendency is to criticize back. ("You're crazy." "You don't know what you're talking about." "You're stupid.") But that rarely leads to anything but a fight. What's more, attacking back may damage your child's self-image . . .

- Because he feels out of control, rather than assertive.
- Because he doesn't know how to respond calmly, with strength.
- Because he feels guilty for lashing out.

Here's a better way to deal with undeserved criticism:

Step One:
Teach your child to empathize with the person who criticizes him—without necessarily agreeing.

YOU: You're lazy.
CHILD: I understand that you feel that way.

YOU: You're late.
CHILD: I know you think I'm late.

CHILD'S FRIEND: You never call me, and I'm your best friend.
CHILD: I know you feel that way.

YOU: You never play with your little sister.
CHILD: I can see why you might feel that way.

CHILD'S FRIEND: You're too tall.
CHILD: I can see that's what you think.

By trying to understand the other person's position, your child is focusing on *the mastery of a new skill* instead of on his hurt.

Tell your child you're going to criticize him unfairly, and ask him to respond by saying that he understands your position. He won't be able to do it perfectly the first time.

YOU: Okay, I'm going to tell you that you never help clear the table. I want you to say that you understand how I'm feeling. Okay, you never help clear the table.
CHILD: What should I say?
YOU: Say, "Mom, I understand how you feel about clean-up."
CHILD: Mom, I understand how you feel about clean-up.
YOU: Great. You empathized with me. You told me that you understood how I'm feeling.

Empathy is a difficult skill to learn, even for an adult. It will take a lot of patience on your part to teach it to your child.

Step Two:

Follow up with the respectful BUT:

"BUT I finished all my chores and all my homework before I turned on the TV."

"BUT I'm not late. It's exactly five o'clock."

"BUT you weren't around all the hours I read to her and played with her. I spend a lot of time with my sister."

"BUT I turned in my paper yesterday, just after George turned in his."

"BUT I like my height just fine."

"BUT it is my turn. I've been waiting in line for twenty minutes."

Use role reversal and behavior rehearsal to teach your child "the respectful BUT."

YOU: Okay, you be me and I'll be you. Go ahead and criticize me, unfairly.

CHILD: You're lazy.

YOU: Okay, I don't think that that's true. But I'm not going to attack back. First I'm going to empathize with you. Then I'm going to state the truth firmly and clearly. Okay, I understand that you think I'm lazy. That's the empathy. BUT, in fact, I did all the dishes and my homework before I went out to play. That was "the respectful BUT." Now I'll criticize you. It's going to be something inaccurate, something you don't deserve. Okay?

CHILD: Okay.

YOU: Okay. You're late. Now remember, you're not late. What are you going to say?

CHILD: I can't remember.

YOU: First, you're going to empathize with me. Say that you understand.

CHILD: Oh, right. Well, I understand that you think I'm late.

YOU: Good. You showed you understood my position, even though you didn't agree with it. Now what?

CHILD: I'm going to give you a BUT.

PARENT: Right.

CHILD: BUT it's just five o'clock, and that was the time we agreed on.

PARENT: Great. Now if I keep disagreeing with you, all you have to do is repeat your "respectful BUT." Okay?

CHILD: Okay.

PARENT: You're late all the time. It seems like you're always late.

CHILD: BUT I'm not late today. It's just five o'clock.

PARENT: Why are you late so often?

CHILD: You feel I'm late a lot. BUT I'm not late today. It's just five o'clock.

PARENT: Terrific. Next time anyone criticizes you unjustly, don't start fighting. Do what we've just done. First show the person that you understand what he's saying. That way, you're lessening the chance that he'll keep arguing, and keeping yourself from feeling weak and defensive.

YOU: Let's try it again.

CHILD: Okay.

PARENT: I'm going to criticize you. The criticism will be inaccurate and undeserved. You never call me, and I'm your best friend.

CHILD: Okay, first I'll empathize. I understand that it feels like I never call you.

PARENT: Great.

CHILD: BUT I call you three times a week. That's not "never."

PARENT: Great. I'm going to keep going. How come you never call me?

CHILD: BUT I call you at least three times a week, and I think that's pretty often.

PARENT: Great.

By empathizing, your child will be disarming his critic without giving in. Then, with "the respectful BUT," he will be deflecting the criticism without having to argue back.

The old way of dealing with criticism:

PARENT: You didn't clean your room.

CHILD: Well, I didn't have time.

PARENT: Of course you didn't have time. You were busy playing that stupid game all day.

CHILD: There's nothing stupid about that game.

PARENT: Well, not the game. But there is something stupid about playing it all day, when you have other things to do. You also didn't walk the dog—I had to do it.

CHILD: I thought you wanted to do it.

PARENT: Believe me, I didn't want to. It just seems that way because I end up doing it all the time. Remember, you promised to do it every day, and you haven't kept your promise.

CHILD: Well, how can I, with all the schoolwork I have to do?

PARENT: Schoolwork? I hate to say this, but I haven't seen you do more than ten minutes of homework a night this entire year.

CHILD: You don't know what you're talking about.

Great for exercising your vocal cords; lousy for your child's self-esteem.

The new way of dealing with criticism:

PARENT: You didn't clean your room.

CHILD: You're right. I didn't, and I'll get to it right now.

Here's what you may be saying:

"Your room is a mess again."
"Your grades are terrible."
"I don't like the kids you're hanging out with."

Instead, try saying:

"From now on, I think it would be good if you cleaned your room every day."
"I think you should do at least three hours of homework every night, in order to improve your grades."
"I'd really like it if you'd call that new girl down the block."

If you've been using criticism to try to change your child's behavior, your child has been hearing put-downs, rather than instructions. And that has almost certainly damaged your child's self-esteem.

Leave criticism out of it.

By leaving the criticism out of it, you will be doing your child—and yourself—a favor. Instead of feeling hurt, defensive, worthless, your child will be able to concentrate on following your wishes.

- *Not* "You eat too much candy" *but* "It would be great if you could stick to one piece a day."
- *Not* "You're not a very good tennis player" *but* "If you'd like, we can spend tomorrow morning practicing your backhand."
- *Not* "You're treating Susan very rudely" *but* "I'd like to talk to you about what you can do to be a better friend to Susan."

Don't criticize when what you really want to do is help.

SUMMARY

Try to criticize your child less often.

Find out (by asking your child) what kinds of criticism he receives.

Create a hierarchy of criticisms, from least to most hurtful.

For deserved criticism:

Teach your child to respond nondefensively, nonargumentatively, nonemotionally.

YOU: You're late again.
CHILD: You're right. I'm late.

Use behavior rehearsal, role reversal, and prompts and cues to teach him the emotional shrug (a feeling of "I hear you, but I'm not letting it hurt me").

For undeserved criticism:

Teach him to empathize with his critics

YOU: You're late again.
CHILD: I understand that you think I'm late.

Then, using role reversal, behavior rehearsal, and prompts and cues, teach him to come back at his critics with the firm, truthful, respectful BUT:

- "BUT I'm really right on time."
- "BUT I have done all my homework."

If your child's critic persists, he should repeat his BUT statement as often as he has to, without raising his voice or criticizing back.

If you've been trying to change your child's behavior using criticism:

Try focusing on the task at hand, without criticizing your child: *Not* "You're terrible for messing up your room again." *but* "I'd like you to begin cleaning your room every night."

7

WITH HEART HELD HIGH: THE RIGHT WAY TO HANDLE TEASING

RACHEL'S STORY

At her new school—a large, impersonal middle school where she knew almost no one—Rachel's classmates couldn't see how intelligent or thoughtful or imaginative she was (and she was all those things). What they saw was a short, plain-looking girl who was underdeveloped for her age, which was ten. And so, for Rachel, the nightmare of being teased had started.

- Kevin, a boy on her school bus, told her, "You're ugly. You're the ugliest girl on the bus."
- Steven, a tall boy in her homeroom, leaned over her and said, "I bet you don't even wear a bra yet."
- A girl whose name she didn't know came up to her at lunch and said, "No boy will ever ask *you* out."
- When the class had to fill out medical forms, someone said,

"I wonder what Rachel is going to put down for 'sex' "—and everybody laughed.

■ A girl in her homeroom told her, "Ha, ha. I bet you haven't even been invited to the dance."

Everywhere Rachel went in her new school, what should have been an exciting time for her was marred by teasing (or the threat of teasing, which felt just as bad).

No doubt there were plenty of people in her school who would have befriended her. But they were scared off by her tormentors. She was left feeling lonely, helpless, and overpowered. In the lunchroom she was frightened to sit down, frightened to look around. The teasers were making her life miserable.

And it wasn't going to stop until she did something about it.

It hadn't taken long for Rachel's parents to find out she was hurting. They were *empathetic* people—when their daughter spoke, they really listened, and they tried to feel what she was feeling. What they heard was that she didn't like her teachers, that she didn't like her classmates, that she wished she could go back to grade school. Rachel didn't say anything about being teased—she was far too embarrassed for that—but her parents guessed. Like a lot of parents, they had memories of being teased themselves.

Gradually, however, Rachel opened up; she told her parents that some of her classmates teased her. She was still too embarrassed to *describe* the teasing, but her parents didn't push. Instead they told her how sorry they were ("We know what it's like to be teased, and we can understand how bad you're feeling.") They told her why children might want to tease her ("They're insecure."), which made her feel a little better, and they told her about people they knew who had been teased as children—and

who turned out to be successful, *popular* adults. That made
Rachel feel more confident about the future. But what about
right now?

Rachel's parents wanted to help their daughter, but they
didn't know how.

They thought about the times they'd been teased as children,
and how they had coped (or tried to).

Between them, Rachel's parents had tried

crying
lying
running away
fighting back
one-upping
tattling
changing their behavior to "suit" their tormentors.

But none of that had dissuaded their tormentors. Rachel's parents knew that if she were to succeed where they had failed,
would have to find a better way to handle teasing.

At a meeting in my office, Rachel's parents told me about their
daughter's situation. I suggested that we teach Rachel to stop
giving her teasers the reaction they wanted. By running away,
crying, or fighting back, she was encouraging them. They *wanted*
to see her upset. Rachel's parents agreed that she should stop
playing into their hands. But, as her father observed, "That's
easier said than done. Rachel knows she should ignore them, but
when the time comes, it's hard not to react."

"Hard," I agreed, "but not impossible." I told Rachel's parents that by using behavior-therapy techniques, I could train her
to feel confident and in control in the face of even the most
hurtful teasing. But first, I said, I had to teach Rachel to be
assertive. Rachel's parents had heard of assertiveness training
for adults, and it scared them. They associated assertiveness

with brashness, and they worried that Rachel would become tough or overbearing.

I responded by giving them my definition of assertiveness:

- Being able to express one's feelings easily.
- Expressing those feelings calmly, not in a hostile or aggressive way.
- Being an active (rather than a passive) participant in life.
- Being straightforward and forthright (in uncomfortable situations), rather than embarrassed or defensive.

I explained that I would be training Rachel to feel stronger. And that strength, I said, would translate into a "quiet confidence" that would dissuade her tormentors.

Rachel's parents arranged for her to see me once a week. At our first session, I asked her how she felt about her new school. She had a hard time answering. She looked confused and angry. (I imagined she felt bad about having to see a therapist. She might have been thinking, "What's wrong with me that I have to see a doctor to make other children like me?") I asked her The Question ("Tell me something you like about yourself"), and she looked down at the floor.

I encouraged Rachel to open up by asking her about her feelings (while being careful not to put words in her mouth).

- "How do you feel about being here with me?"
- "How do you feel about your classmates?"
- "How do you feel when someone teases you?"

I suggested feelings she might have (*always* giving her a choice of answers): Are you feeling sad? Happy? Upset? Calm? Does going to school make you anxious? Relaxed? Unhappy? Excited?

Rachel seemed to become more comfortable as the session

went on. She began to smile, and, eventually, she started telling me some of her feelings.

- "I don't like my school."
- "The other students aren't nice."
- "I feel mad, because my other school was so much better."

Each time she answered, I praised her for being so open and I empathized. ("I understand that you feel bad about that.")

At the end of the session, I gave her a notebook, and I asked her to write down two or three feelings every day. I suggested that she try to begin each feeling with "I":

"I wish I didn't have to go to school."
(*Not* "School is terrible.")
"I'm glad my parents are helping me."
(*Not* "My parents are nice to do this.")
"I'm upset about giving up time each week to see a therapist."
(*Not* "Therapy is a drag.")
"I feel tired."
(*Not* "This is exhausting.")

I told Rachel that starting every sentence with "I" was the best way to make sure that she was expressing her own feelings, not somebody else's.

The next week, Rachel came back with two pages of feelings, which she read to me. I responded with positive reinforcement. ("Great." "Wonderful." "You're doing a good job." "Thanks for telling me that." "I'm glad that you could write that down." "Most of your feelings start with 'I,' which is terrific. Thanks for doing it that way.")

At the end of the session, I asked Rachel which of her parents she felt more comfortable talking to. She immediately said, "My mother." So I asked her to express a couple of feelings each day to her mother. I told Rachel that if she needed practice, she could express her feelings to herself, in private. Or she could try them out on her dog, or a doll, a stuffed animal, or even to the mirror—before expressing them to her mother.

The next week, Rachel came back with a list of the feelings she had expressed to her mother, everything from "I hate this brand of jelly" to "I wish I could go to a new school." I praised her for doing her "homework," and I asked her if she felt ready to express some feelings to her father (whom she found more intimidating than her mother).

The following week, Rachel told me that she had expressed at least one feeling to her father every day. I praised her and asked her to continue expressing feelings to people—people like her brother, her best friend, and her teacher. She agreed to try. Expressing feelings was becoming easier for Rachel.

Here are some of the feelings Rachel expressed during the next few weeks:

- To her brother: "I wish you would share your toys with me as often as I share mine with you."
- To her mother: "I'm really glad you pick me up every day after school."
- To her teacher: "I'm learning a lot in this class, and I'm excited."
- To her friend Jean: "It would be great if you'd come over to my house this weekend. I have a lot of new things I want to show you."
- To a girl in school, whom she was just getting to know: "I wish we had a longer lunch, so we would have more time to talk."

The next time I saw her, Rachel's notebook was filled with feelings—feelings she was now expressing freely for the first time in her life.

I told Rachel I felt she was ready to work on specific techniques to combat teasing. First I asked her to think of a time in her life when she felt competent, in control, and on top of the world. Rachel said, "Well, when I starred in the school play last year, and I got a standing ovation from the entire school, I felt terrific."

I told Rachel that whenever talking about teasing made her uncomfortable, she should imagine herself receiving that ovation. "Just put whatever's bothering you out of your mind, and think about that time when you felt really special."

Then I asked her to tell me about the things people said when they teased her. I knew Rachel would feel uncomfortable reeling them off. So I suggested that she give me only one example at a time. In between, I said, she could think about the school play, or about any other pleasant subject. I was making sure Rachel had a "security blanket," a "comforter" to grab onto if the discussion of teasing made her overly anxious.

Gradually she began to tell me some of the things people said when they teased her. I responded empathetically ("It must really hurt you when someone says that."), and I praised her for confiding in me. Then we chatted about her friends, the teachers she liked, her favorite TV show. Every once in a while I stopped, and I told her to relax, close her eyes, and think about her triumph in the school play.

Then I told Rachel that in order to help her, I needed to learn how she reacted when people teased her. I asked her to play a game—in which I would pretend to tease her, and she would pretend to respond. Every few minutes, I said, we would take a break to talk about a more enjoyable subject.

ME: Okay, I'm the girl in your homeroom. I bet you haven't been invited to the dance.

RACHEL: *(Looking crushed)* What dance?

ME: Ha, ha. She didn't even know about the dance.

(Rachel still looks crushed)

ME: Rachel, you showed that girl that she could hurt you. You gave her what she wanted, and she'll probably try to hurt you again. We'll work on that in a few minutes. Now tell me more about that movie that you said you liked so much . . .

Over the course of an hour, we also acted out these scenes:

ME: Now I'm another kid in your school. I bet Rachel doesn't know what to put down for "sex."

(Rachel looks devastated)

ME: Look at the crybaby.

(Rachel still looks hurt)

ME: Now I'll be Steven. I bet Rachel doesn't even wear a bra yet.

RACHEL: That's none of your business.

ME: Oh, yeah, it is if I say it is.

RACHEL: Is not.

ME: Is too.

I praised Rachel for being brave enough to play along. Then I told her I wanted her to tease me, and to see how *I* reacted.

RACHEL: Boy, you are stupid. You are stupid and ugly.

(I am silent, expressionless, heart held high)

(Rachel is silent, has nothing to say)

ME: You see how that worked. I ignored you. I just looked you in the eye, and I didn't look hurt. I sat up straight, with my heart held high. Being teased didn't seem to bother me at all. And because of that, you had nothing to say.

Then I asked Rachel to do what I had done. Over the next half hour, I teased her half a dozen times. Each time she said nothing. When she looked hurt, I said I understood how she felt, but I asked her to try not to show it. When she succeeded, I praised her.

ME: I bet you haven't been invited to the dance.
(*Rachel is silent*)
ME: Great. You didn't react at all. Let's try it again.
RACHEL: Okay. Tease me.
ME: You're so ugly, Rachel.
(*Rachel is silent*)
ME: Terrific. But you looked a little hurt. Let's do it again.

I asked Rachel to focus on another role model: herself, during her triumphant curtain call. From now on, I said, when I teased her, I wanted her to think about her "moment of glory."

Then I teased her again. This time she looked me right in the eye and said nothing. She seemed confident and completely unruffled. Rachel was perfecting the *emotional shrug*—a look of confidence and calm indifference, a look that says, "Your teasing doesn't matter."

That week she tried the emotional shrug whenever she was teased in school. It hadn't been easy, she later told me. Sometimes she had cried, or argued, or run away. But most of the time she had stood up straight, looked her tormentor in the eye (with indifference rather than defiance), and shrugged—all the while thinking about her triumph in the play. Already, she reported, her classmates were teasing her less often.

I congratulated her, and then I began teaching her another

important skill. In addition to using the emotional shrug, I said, I wanted her to *agree* with the person who teased her (whenever agreeing made sense). Agreeing with her attacker would make her seem (and feel) supremely self-assured. And it would leave the teaser speechless.

We rehearsed the response together:

ME: I bet you weren't even invited to the dance. Now say, "You're right, I haven't been invited to the dance." Remember to make eye contact, and don't look hurt.

RACHEL: You're right, I haven't been invited to the dance.

ME: Great. You did that just right. You stood up to the person who teased you. You didn't let the teasing get under your skin. How did it feel?

RACHEL: Good.

ME: Now I'm going to try it again. Rachel, I bet you don't even wear a bra yet. Ha, ha. Now agree with me, and say, "You're right, I don't wear a bra yet." And don't look hurt.

RACHEL: You're right, I don't wear a bra yet.

ME: Terrific. How did it feel to do that?

RACHEL: It felt good. I'm not crying or anything.

ME: If you're upset, take a break and think about the school play.

RACHEL: I don't need to. I feel fine.

ME: That's wonderful.

I asked Rachel to keep responding to teasing with the emotional shrug and, if possible, to agree with her teaser. Two weeks later, I saw her again. She told me she was being teased less—and that when she was, she didn't feel helpless; she felt stronger, more in control, and more assertive.

I practiced with her one more time. I repeated some of the most vicious things people had said to her. And, through it all, she looked me in the eye with what appeared to be total indifference. And she agreed with me (her teaser) whenever she could, which stopped me in my tracks.

Rachel was ready to deal with teasing on her own. From then on, I talked to her about once a month. Thinking of our conversations as "refresher courses," I reminded her to be assertive, to use the emotional shrug, and to agree with her tormentors whenever she could. I praised her for making so much progress.

A year later Rachel wrote me a letter, telling me that no one teased her anymore. And she didn't think it was because *they* had changed. She thought it was because of her self-confidence, her assertiveness—and her wonderful emotional shrug.

Every child is a candidate for teasing. Children are teased for being different—which can mean almost anything:

Tall
Short
Thin
Fat
Smart
Not smart
Black
White
Wears white socks
Wears black socks
Eats meat
Doesn't eat meat

Wears glasses
Wears braces
Plays with boys
Plays with girls
Plays by himself
Reads books
Takes ballet
Poor
Rich

If you've ever been a victim of teasing, you know it isn't "all in good fun." Even in its mildest forms, teasing is hurtful; at its most severe, it can leave a child emotionally scarred.

Teasing, not surprisingly, is an enemy of self-esteem. When he's teased, your child hears bad things about himself from people who seem powerful, important. What's more, being teased—and not knowing how to handle it—may make your child feel helpless, incompetent, and insecure. Unfortunately those negative feelings may outlive the teasing—by decades.

There is no perfect defense against teasing. But by using the techniques in this chapter, you will be able to protect your child's self-esteem from much of the devastation that teasing can bring.

To do that, you will need to help your child feel competent and in control, no matter how viciously he's teased. He'll need to convince his tormentors that their teasing rolls right off him. He'll need to feel as powerful to his teasers as they feel to him.

Once your child acts strong, he'll start to feel strong. (As is so often the case, the feeling will follow the doing.) And his tormentors, defeated in their mission to unnerve him, will surrender.

Perhaps you knew, before you bought this book, that the best way to handle teasing is to "not let it upset you." Perhaps you've even told your child that. But telling him isn't enough. Your child can't become strong just because he wants to. He needs to learn specific techniques to stand firm in the face of teasing— techniques that you can teach him.

Assertiveness

First, your child will have to learn to be assertive. Not aggressive. Not obnoxious. Just quietly, confidently assertive.

Assertiveness doesn't mean brashness, shrillness, or lack of consideration. It is simply the ability to express oneself with confidence. People who are truly assertive *don't need to be* aggressive.

Assertiveness is competence in social situations. It is knowing the best way to handle encounters that have the potential to make you feel incompetent or anxious.

By learning to be assertive, your child will be learning to push anxiety aside.

Before learning the specific techniques for dealing with teasing later in this chapter, your child must learn how to be assertive. Set aside ten minutes a day, perhaps right after school, or just before his bedtime, for "assertiveness training."

Step One:

Ask your child The Question—"Tell me something you like about yourself." If he answers freely—if he can talk about his strengths without embarrassment—he is well on his way to becoming assertive.

If he can't answer The Question, you'll want to practice the techniques in chapter 2. Take your time. Encourage your child by telling him what *you* like about him. And when he does answer

The Question, give him positive reinforcement: "That's terrific. Thanks for telling me about that."

When your child can answer The Question without hesitation, go on to step 2.

Step Two:

Give your child a notebook, and ask her to write down three "I" statements a day. Give her some examples:

- "I am warm." (*Not* "It's warm in here.")
- "I'm mad at Shirley." (*Not* "Shirley isn't a good friend.")
- "I'm bored in school this year." (*Not* "School is boring.")
- "I love playing tennis." (*Not* "Tennis is fun.")

Being able to make "I" statements is an important part of assertive expression. *Every time he uses the word "I," your child is acknowledging his own importance.*

Step Three:

Encourage your child to begin expressing feelings. To get him started, you may want to give him choices: Do you feel tired? sad? happy? mad? glad? sorry?

Or you may want to suggest situations: How did you feel after school today? after the movie? after your father yelled at you? when you won at miniature golf?

Step Four:

Ask your child to recall a time when she felt competent and in control—a scene she can return to (mentally) when she becomes tired or anxious about teasing.

PARENT: Can you remember a time when you felt on top of the world?

STEVE, eight: Last week, when I was playing kickball and I scored three times.

Then, using empathy and positive reinforcement, encourage your child to describe the scene in greater detail.

PARENT: Great. That sounds terrific. I'd like to know more.
STEVE: Well, everyone told me I was the best player on the team, and that we won the game because of me.
PARENT: Great. Do you remember anything else?
STEVE: Yeah. Gary said he wanted to play with me all the time, because I was the best player. And I really like Gary.
PARENT: That must have felt great.

Whenever your child seems uncomfortable with the discussion, give him a minute to "return" to his "moment of glory."

PARENT: Steve, relax and think about the time you scored that goal in kickball. I'm sure it will make you feel better.
STEVE: Uh-huh!

Step Five:
Ask your child to tell you how comfortable (or uncomfortable) each of her feelings makes her.
Use her answers to develop a hierarchy of feelings.

JENNIFER'S HIERARCHY OF FEELINGS
From most to least comfortable:
1. I feel sleepy.
2. I feel warm.
3. I feel excited about going.
4. I'm scared.

5. I'm worried.
6. I feel proud of the way I did that.
7. I feel lonely.
8. I wish I were pretty.
9. I feel left out.
10. I feel rejected because Jill didn't call me.

Then ask your child how comfortable she would be expressing those feelings to

- her mother
- her father
- her English teacher
- her sister or brother
- her principal
- her best friend
- and so on.

"How about Mrs. Green? Are you comfortable talking to her?"
"How about Jason next door?"
Use her answers to create another hierarchy.

JENNIFER'S HIERARCHY OF PEOPLE TO EXPRESS FEELINGS TO

From easiest to hardest:
1. My doll
2. Mom
3. Dad
4. Sandra (sister)
5. Mrs. Green (teacher)
6. Jason (big boy next door)
7. Sven (bully on school bus)

Encourage your child to express her feelings to the people on the list. At first she may want to express an easy feeling ("I'm excited.") to someone she finds easy to talk to (her best friend). That's okay for now. (Give her plenty of encouragement and positive reinforcement.)

Gradually encourage her to work her way up to "harder" feelings—and more intimidating people. Don't rush; let her decide when to take the next step. (And tell her to stop before she gets to anyone who will put her down or tease her.)

Once you feel your child can express a variety of feelings to a variety of people, you can begin teaching her the specific techniques for dealing with teasing.

Know the enemy.

To help your child learn to handle teasing, you're going to have to know

- who teases her
- what they say to her
- how she reacts.

Talking about teasing with your child won't be easy, for two reasons:

1. She may be ashamed, embarrassed, scared.
2. *You* may be ashamed, embarrassed, scared. (It's painful for you to think about your child being teased.)

If *you* need encouragement, close your eyes and picture someone you love giving *you* positive reinforcement. ("Darling, it's so great that you're making an effort to help Jennifer deal with teasing.")

There are lots of ways to draw your child out:

- Talk about the times you were teased.
- Talk about people you know who were teased—and how well they turned out.
- Soothe your child with healthy doses of empathy and positive reinforcement. If she becomes uncomfortable at any point, tell her to close her eyes and think about her "moment of glory."
- Talk in a place where your child is comfortable. Play music she likes. Let her hold a favorite doll or teddy bear. Anything you can do to relax your child will make the time you spend together that much more productive.
- Stop every few minutes to talk about something more pleasant than teasing. (If your child can look forward to a few minutes of *enjoyable* conversation, he'll have an easier time discussing teasing.)

Tell your child that you need to know as much as you can about the people who tease him:

YOU: Okay. I'll play you. You be the bully. Close your eyes and imagine the situation. Now, go ahead and tease me.
CHILD: You're stupid. You're stupid. You're sooooo stupid.
YOU: Okay. Terrific. Now that I know what that bully says to you, it will be much easier for me to help you.

Next, tell your child that to help him handle teasing effectively, you're going to have to see how he handles it now. Tell him you're going to play a game: you'll play the teaser, and he'll show you how he reacts.

YOU: Okay, I'll be that big boy on the school bus this time. I'll tell you that you're stupid, and you react the way you normally would. You're stupid. You're stupid. You're sooooo stupid. Now react the way you normally would.

CHILD: Leave me alone, you jerk.

YOU: Great. It's really important for me to see how you react.

Teach your child the emotional shrug.

The emotional shrug is a way of saying, "I don't care. It doesn't matter to me."

The emotional shrug is synonymous with the words "sure," "whatever," or "same difference."

To teach your child the emotional shrug, you may need to reverse roles. Tell your child to play the part of the teaser. That way, you can demonstrate the desired behavior.

YOU: You be Bobby and I'll be you. Now tell me what Bobby says that makes you mad.

CHILD: You're the worst athlete in the class.

YOU: I am not.

CHILD: You are too, you sissy.

YOU: You see, I didn't handle that right. I argued with you, and you argued back. Let's try it again. This time I won't give you the reaction you want. I'm going to shrug inside, and I'm going to say to myself, "So what? Big deal." Go ahead, tease me again.

CHILD: You're the worst athlete in the class. You throw a baseball like a girl.

(*You are silent, looking straight ahead, heart held high*)

(*Child is silent*)

YOU: You see, it worked. I gave you an emotional shrug, and there was nothing left for you to say.

Reverse roles, giving your child a chance to try the emotional shrug.

YOU: This time, I'm going to tease you. When I do,

- Don't say a word.
- Stand up straight and face me.
- Look me in the eye.
- Don't cry, turn around, or run away.
- Hold your head—and your heart—high.

CHILD: Okay.

YOU: Here goes. Boy, are you stupid. Now don't say a word. Just look at me like you don't care.

(Child is silent)

YOU: Good. But you looked a little hurt. Try not to next time. Try to feel like, "I don't even have time to listen to you. I don't care what you're saying." Now, let's try it again.

If he wants to, your child can *really* shrug. The goal is to learn to shrug inside, but any kind of shrug is a good first step.

It may take three or four weeks for your child to learn the emotional shrug. He may have a strong impulse to fight back ("It takes one to know one." "No, you're the stupid one.") Staying silent in the face of teasing takes restraint—and that kind of restraint can only come with practice.

Teach your child to agree.

To really unnerve his teasers, your child can do the one thing they'd never expect: agree with them. Crying, running away, or fighting with his tormentors makes your child feel weak and defensive and encourages the teasers by giving them what they want. Agreeing with them makes him feel strong and in control and discourages the teasers.

Of course, there will be plenty of times your child won't be able to agree:

"You're the ugliest girl in the class."
"You're a sissy."

But more often than not he will be able to agree:

"You have to wear a hearing aid. Hah, hah."
"You're the shortest boy in the school."
"My mother says your parents are divorced. Your father doesn't even live with you anymore. Do you hear that, guys? His father doesn't even live with him anymore."

Reverse roles again. Have your child play the teaser. This will teach you the language, the vocabulary of your child's tormentors and give you a chance to demonstrate the desired response to teasing.

YOU: Okay, I'll be you, and you be that girl at school who teases you. Tell me what she says that makes you feel bad.
CHILD: Ha, ha. Your clothes are funny.
YOU: Oh, yeah. So what if they are?
CHILD: Well, you look weird. Everyone says you look weird.
YOU: See, I was defensive. That wasn't the right thing to do. Tease me again. This time, I'll agree with you.
CHILD: Ha, ha. Your clothes are funny.
YOU: You're right. My clothes are different.
(Child is silent)
YOU: You see, it worked. I agreed with you, so you had nothing left to say.

Now take the role of the teaser.

YOU: Okay, I'm going to tease you now. You got a D on your test. Ha, ha. Now agree with me. Say, "You're right. I got a D."

CHILD: You're right, I got a D.

YOU: What a jerk. I said you got a D, and you agreed with me. Ha, ha.

CHILD: I did get a D.

YOU: Great. I'm stuck. I'm not getting anywhere. You did that just right.

CHILD: Thanks.

YOU: If you had said you didn't get a D, I would have called you a liar, and we would have started fighting. This way, you took control. I was left with nothing to say. Let's try it again. I'll tease you again. You're the shortest kid in the class. You're a midget. Now agree that you are short.

CHILD: You're right. I am the shortest kid in this class.

YOU: Terrific. I have nothing left to say.

Ask your child to try agreeing with "real" teasers. (Doing this with real teasers will be difficult at first, but it will become easier with practice.) Every day or two, ask him when he was last teased, and how he dealt with it. If he used the emotional shrug, or agreed with the person who teased him—praise him for learning a new (and better) way to handle teasing.

SUMMARY

Assertiveness:

Ask your child The Question—"Tell me something you like about yourself." If he answers freely, go on to the next step. (If not, you may need to go back to chapter 3.)

Ask your child to write down feelings—beginning with the word "I."

Ask your child to recall a time when he felt happy and in control. (Keep that scene in reserve, for your child to "return to" any time he becomes anxious.)

Make a hierarchy (a list, from easy to hard) of your child's feelings and another hierarchy of people to whom your child may want to express those feelings.

Ask your child to begin expressing feelings to people with whom she feels comfortable. Gradually have her work her way up to harder and harder feelings and to people she feels less and less comfortable talking to. (Help her along with empathy and positive reinforcement.)

Specific techniques for dealing with teasing:

Learn the language of your child's tormentors. Use role reversal. ("I'll be you. Now tease me the way that boy in school teases you.")

Learn how your child responds to teasing. ("Okay. I'm going to tease you now. Let's see how you respond.")

Teach your child "the emotional shrug"—a look of "Who cares; I'm above that; I don't have to listen to that; nothing you say matters."

Teach your child to *agree* with the people who tease her (when it makes sense to do so): "You're right, I did drop the ball." "That's right, I got a D on the test."

Demonstrate the correct behavior for your child. ("Okay, go ahead and tease me, and watch how I respond.")

Use cues ("Okay, it's time for you to respond.") and prompts ("Here's what you should say now . . . ").

Give your child lots of empathy ("It must feel awful when he says that.") and positive reinforcement ("Great, you did that right.").

8

▼▲

REJECTION WITHOUT
PAIN (ALMOST)

ANDREW'S STORY

Just after his eleventh birthday, Andrew suffered what for him was the worst possible rejection: his father left home to live with another woman two hundred miles away. Since then Andrew had spent part of every morning in his father's study, surrounded by his father's things. Andrew's mother often awoke to find him there, looking despondent. When she tried to console him, Andrew said that he would never be happy again, no matter what, and that she shouldn't even try to help him!

In school his work had become careless; his teachers reported that he was only going through the motions. And his friends didn't know what to make of his behavior: most of the time, he looked like he wanted to cry.

Andrew's mother was surprised by the severity of her son's reaction, and it scared her. (She was already depressed, and Andrew's problems added to her burden.) She desperately wanted to find a way to help him. That's when she contacted me about my self-esteem program. She asked me if I would work with Andrew, and I said I would.

There was only one problem: Andrew's father wouldn't let him see a therapist. In heated conversations with Andrew's mother, he said, "Andrew's a big boy now, and he should deal with this problem himself. He's not the first child whose parents have gotten divorced."

But Andrew's mother, who saw what her son was going through, was sure he needed help. And since she couldn't bring her son to me, she decided to bring my techniques to him. She asked me if I would train her to work with Andrew at home. I said I would, and I began showing her how to help her son deal with the pain of rejection. Each week I taught her a few more techniques, and she reported on his progress.

She began her "program" one morning when she found Andrew moping around his father's study. She didn't push him to participate. She simply told him that she wanted to help him feel better. He said, "If you can't bring my father back, I don't know how you can help me." She said that although she couldn't bring his father back, she would be able to help him feel less horrible about his father's leaving.

The next day, Andrew's mother sat him down in a comfortable place and asked him if he'd ever felt rejection. Andrew said he didn't know what she meant by rejection, so she gave him some examples:

- The way you feel when someone you know gives a party, and you're not invited.
- The way you feel when someone doesn't want to be your friend.
- The way you feel when your father says he won't be living with you anymore.

She told Andrew that everyone experiences rejection, and that most people have difficulty talking about it freely, but that it's better when people can discuss it.

Still Andrew seemed reticent, so she began telling him about rejections she had suffered. First she talked about "little" rejections—friends who hadn't shown up, clients who had dropped her. Later she began to describe how the divorce had affected her. Andrew, who had never heard her talk about rejection before, seemed surprised that someone as grown-up as his mother would feel the way she did about rejection. (In fact, he realized, his mother's feelings were a lot like his.)

Then she asked him again, "Have you ever felt rejection?" This time, Andrew wasn't afraid to answer.

- He told her about a girl in school who said she didn't want to be his friend anymore.
- He told her about a teacher who sometimes didn't call on him for hours, no matter how often he raised his hand.
- Eventually he told her about how his father's leaving had affected him. "It felt like I had done something wrong, like I was being punished."

Each time Andrew told his mother about a rejection, she empathized and praised him. Sometimes she talked about times she'd been rejected as a child:

ANDREW: There are days when no one wants to play with me at recess.
MOM: When I was your age, that used to happen to me a lot.
ANDREW: Really?
MOM: Sure. That kind of thing can happen to anyone.
ANDREW: What did you do?
MOM: Eventually I found a whole new group of friends.
ANDREW: Maybe that will happen to me.

Sometimes, when it made sense, she encouraged him to respond to the person who rejected him.

ANDREW: My teacher didn't call on me all day.
MOM: Wouldn't it be a good idea for you to stay after class and ask her why?
ANDREW: I'm not sure.
MOM: Well, you might feel better if, instead of just worrying about what happened, you do something about it.
ANDREW: I guess you're right.
MOM: If you want me to help you decide what to say, I will.
ANDREW: Great.

Sometimes she even talked about how she felt when *she* rejected people:

ANDREW: My friend Randy hasn't called me back in three days.
MOM: What do you think that means?
ANDREW: He doesn't like me anymore.
MOM: Well, sometimes I can't call someone back for a couple of days because I'm really busy, or I'm not feeling well. Hasn't that ever happened to you?
ANDREW: Yeah, sometimes.
MOM: So if you don't call someone back right away, it doesn't always mean you don't like him, does it?
ANDREW: No.
MOM: So maybe you shouldn't assume Randy doesn't like you.
ANDREW: Maybe not.

In the course of their discussions, Andrew's mother asked him how bad each rejection felt. At first, they used words like "okay" and "not so great" and "horrible"; but gradually they switched to a one-to-ten scale:

"That sounds pretty mild. Do you think it's a two?"

"Boy, that really hurt you. What number would you give that? A six or a seven?"

Sometimes Andrew talked about imagined or "anticipatory" rejections: situations that frightened him, although they hadn't happened and probably never would. When she made Andrew's "hierarchy," his mother included those rejections, which she knew were very "real" to Andrew.

ANDREW'S REJECTION HIERARCHY

From least to most severe:

1. I raise my hand and the teacher doesn't call on me.
2. My teacher doesn't call on me all day.
3. Josh can't play with me tonight.
4. (Anticipatory) Josh can't play with me for a couple of weeks.
5. (Anticipatory) I sit down in the cafeteria, and no one wants to sit with me. I end up eating alone.
6. (Anticipatory) Josh tells me he doesn't want to be my friend anymore, ever.
7. (Anticipatory) Josh has a party, and I'm the only person in my class who's not invited.
8. (Anticipatory) I sit down next to a friend in the cafeteria, and he gets up and moves away.
9. My father says he's thinking of leaving.
10. My father leaves.

She told Andrew that she was going to teach him to handle the milder rejections (1–5 on his hierarchy) with an "emotional shrug," a way of feeling, of saying to himself, "This isn't so bad. It isn't pleasant, but I can live with it."

MOM: Can you tell me about the first item on your list?

ANDREW: Well, sometimes, when I raise my hand, and my teacher doesn't call on me, I get really angry. Sometimes it goes on for hours.

MOM: Okay, I know how painful that can be. But I'm going to show you how to give it an emotional shrug. Are you willing to try?

ANDREW: Yes.

MOM: Okay. Now you can really shrug, like this (*She shrugs broadly*), or you can shrug inside—whichever way makes you feel better.

ANDREW: Okay.

MOM: Well then, I want you to imagine that you're in class, and you've had your hand up for a long time, and your teacher hasn't called on you.

ANDREW: Okay, I'm imagining that scene.

MOM: And then, instead of feeling hurt, I want you to say to yourself, "This is no big deal. It's not great, but she'll probably call on me some other time. It doesn't mean she doesn't like me. I can live with this." Okay?

ANDREW: Okay. I'm trying.

MOM: Great. What are you thinking?

ANDREW: That I can live with this. I'm thinking, what's the big deal if she doesn't call on me this once?

MOM: Did you feel like you were shrugging inside?

ANDREW: Uh-huh.

MOM: Wonderful. I know this is new for you, and you're doing really well. Congratulations.

(*The next day*)

MOM: Remember how you did that emotional shrug? Well, I want you to practice it some more.

ANDREW: Okay.

MOM: Let's try the time Josh told you, "I can't play with you tonight." How did that make you feel?

ANDREW: Really awful.

MOM: I know how much that kind of thing can hurt. But if you do an emotional shrug, it will probably feel better. Do you remember how?

ANDREW: I don't think so.

MOM: Okay, how about if I try playing Josh, and let's see how you react. Okay? Hi, Andrew. I'm sorry, but I just can't play with you tonight. I have other plans.

(Andrew looks crushed)

MOM: Try not to look so hurt. Look me in the eye, and try to act more in control. Just say, "Okay, maybe we'll get together another time." I want you to feel like you're shrugging inside.

ANDREW: Okay, maybe we'll get together another time.

MOM: Did you feel like you were shrugging?

ANDREW: I'm trying.

MOM: Great. Now, what were you saying to yourself just then?

ANDREW: I don't know.

MOM: Try saying something like, "I really miss Josh, but this isn't the end of the world. There are other people I can see."

ANDREW: This definitely isn't the end of the world. There are lots of other people I can see.

MOM: Good.

ANDREW: Guess what? I felt like I was shrugging inside.

MOM: Great.

Two weeks later, after many more practice sessions, Andrew's mother felt he was ready to start using the "emotional shrug" in "real-life" situations. Andrew said he'd try, and two days later, he reported this incident to his mother:

ANDREW: Mrs. Granger didn't call on me again. I was angry at first. But then I said to myself, "This is no big deal. I mean, she'll call on me another day. This isn't anything to lose sleep over."

MOM: Terrific. Sounds like you have the emotional shrug down pat. Let me hear about another one.

ANDREW: Well, a lot of my friends had a party last week, but I wasn't invited.

MOM: How did that make you feel?

ANDREW: Awful. I felt like going home and never coming back to school. I felt worthless.

MOM: What did you do?

ANDREW: Well, I stayed mad for a while. But then I remembered the emotional shrug you taught me, and I tried it. I just decided that I can't be invited to every single party. So I started thinking about all the good things that have happened with my friends over the years, and I stopped thinking about rejection. I just put it out of my mind.

MOM: Terrific.

Once Andrew was successfully using the emotional shrug for "milder" rejections, his mother began working with him on more serious, deeply hurtful rejections (6–10 on his list).

Andrew's mother wanted him to replace rejections in his mind with *un-rejections:*

- That his father left was a rejection.
- That his father still came to see him was an un-rejection.
- That Josh didn't want to be his friend was a rejection.
- That Douglas wanted to be his friend was an un-rejection.

She wanted Andrew to know there were a lot of un-rejections in his life. So she asked him to begin keeping a record of

- all the people who like him
- everyone who comes over to talk to him
- everyone who sits down next to him
- everyone who compliments him
- every phone call he gets from his father
- every time his father comes to see him
- every time his father says, "Andrew, I love you."

Within a week, Andrew had written down more than fifty un-rejections. His mother asked him to keep the list with him, and to look at it whenever he felt rejected. Andrew said he would.

But Andrew was still moping around his father's study. His mother could tell that Andrew was still anxious about the serious rejections on his list—so anxious, in fact, that her message about un-rejections wasn't really getting through. I told her that she would have to "calm him down" before her words could have the impact she had hoped for.

I had taught Andrew's mother a series of simple relaxation techniques (similar to but less complex than the ones I use with patients), and now she was ready to try them on her son. She told him that she wanted to make him less upset, to "lower the temperature of his emotions," and that she had learned a way to do that. She told him to think of what they were doing as a kind of game. He seemed unsure of what would happen, but he told her he would "try it."

Andrew's mother praised him for cooperating, and then she asked Andrew about the first serious rejection on his list (number 6). He said the thought of Josh telling him, "Andrew, I don't want to be your friend anymore, ever," made him want to run away and cry.

MOM: That's not a situation you can shrug off. Just thinking about it is painful. But I think I can show you how to lessen the pain.

ANDREW: Okay.

MOM: Okay, I'm going to show you how to become more relaxed about the thought of Josh rejecting you.

ANDREW: Okay.

MOM: Okay. Now lie down in the position that's most comfortable for you. Close your eyes. Think about relaxing. I want you to imagine yourself becoming as relaxed as a wet noodle.

ANDREW: Okay.

MOM: Okay, keep thinking about your entire body becoming as relaxed as a wet noodle.

ANDREW: Okay.

MOM: Now, I want you to make a fist. Make it as tight as you can. And then release your fist, and just think about your fingers relaxing, and your hand relaxing. Study the contrast between your tight fist and how relaxed your hand is now.

ANDREW: Okay.

MOM: Now I want you to tighten the muscles in your face. Make a frown. Frown really hard. And now just release all of that, and let your face just relax. Relax your forehead. Your eye muscles. Your jaw muscles. Just picture your face becoming totally relaxed.

ANDREW: Okay, that feels good.

MOM: Now I want you to picture Josh saying he doesn't want to be your friend anymore.

ANDREW: Okay.

MOM: How does that feel?

ANDREW: Upsetting.

MOM: Does it feel as bad as before?

ANDREW: No, it isn't as bad.

MOM: That's good. That means you're getting more relaxed about it.

ANDREW: I guess you're right.

MOM: Okay, now that you're a little more relaxed, I want you to think about all the other people who are your friends, and I want you to realize that lots of other people haven't rejected you.

ANDREW: Okay.

MOM: Who are some of the people who are still your friends?

ANDREW: Well, there's Sharon, and Allen, and David.

MOM: Great. I want you to think about them. Do you think they still like you?

ANDREW: Yeah, I know they do.

MOM: Great. Keep thinking about Sharon and Allen and David, and how much they all like you.

ANDREW: Okay.

MOM: Take a minute, and just keep thinking about them. *(After a pause)* Now erase that scene. I want you to relax some more.

ANDREW: Okay, it's erased.

MOM: Great. Now think about becoming a wet noodle again.

ANDREW: Okay.

MOM: I want you to focus on another part of your body—this time, try your shoulders. Keep thinking about how totally relaxed they are.

ANDREW: Okay.

MOM: Are you relaxed?

ANDREW: Yes.

MOM: Very relaxed?

ANDREW: Yes.

MOM: Good. Now I want you to think about Josh rejecting you again.

ANDREW: Okay.

MOM: How does that feel?

ANDREW: Okay.

MOM: Are you still upset?

ANDREW: Not as much.

MOM: You don't feel like crying this time, do you?

ANDREW: No. I realize that I have lots of other friends, and they like me a lot.

MOM: Great. I'm glad you could realize that. I think when you were really upset before, it was hard for you to admit that.

ANDREW: I guess it was.

MOM: I'm so glad you feel better.

Gradually Andrew's mother worked her way up to the most painful rejection on Andrew's list.

To help Andrew relax, she lowered the lights and put on his favorite music in the background, and she had him sit in a big, comfortable chair. Then she relaxed him by having him tense, and then release, his fist, and then tense, and release, his facial muscles. And then she said, "Now count your fingers without moving them, and study the warmth in the tips of your fingers." When Andrew let her know that he was deeply relaxed, she asked him to picture himself sitting in his father's study, surrounded by all his father's things:

MOM: Are you picturing that, Andrew?

ANDREW: Yes.

MOM: How does it feel?

ANDREW: Horrible. It's really painful. I feel sick.

MOM: Okay, we're going to work on that right now. Erase the scene completely, and then I'm going to relax you again.

ANDREW: Okay, it's erased.

MOM: Good. Now do you remember how you relaxed the other day?

ANDREW: Yes.

MOM: Let's try it again. I want you to relax. This time, why don't you imagine a scoop of ice cream as it melts. Just focus on it melting . . . melting . . . melting . . . You can even imagine yourself licking the drips. Imagine it's your favorite flavor. Are you feeling more relaxed?

ANDREW: Yes.

MOM: Good. Now try something else. I want you to say the word *calm* to yourself slowly as you breathe out. Say it over and over again each time you exhale. "Calm . . . calm . . . calm . . ." Keep exhaling and saying that to yourself slowly.

ANDREW: Okay, I'm doing it.

Then Andrew's mother had him tense, and then release, his fist, and tense, and then release, his facial muscles, just as he had done before:

MOM: Now count your toes without moving them. And then study the bottoms of your feet—with your eyes closed. Study any feelings, anything at all that you notice about the bottoms of your feet.

(Two minutes later)

MOM: How do you feel?

ANDREW: Really relaxed.

MOM: Great. Now I can talk to you about your father. I want you to understand that he hasn't rejected you. He rejected me. Look at how far he drives every weekend to see you. It's almost two hundred miles, and he does it just to see you.

ANDREW: That's true.

MOM: Do you understand that his leaving had nothing to do with you? It's me he left. Your father still loves you, and there are lots of ways he shows that.

ANDREW: Well, how?

MOM: You tell me.

ANDREW: He comes to see me. He talks to me. He does things with me. He hugs me. *(Tearfully)* I miss him, Mom.

MOM: I know you do. But he's not rejecting you. He loves you and he always will. Do you know that?

ANDREW: Yes, I do.

MOM: I'm glad you understand that. We both love you, Andrew.

ANDREW: I know that.

MOM: Good. Now, are you still feeling relaxed?

ANDREW: Yeah, I don't feel bad at all.

MOM: Great. Now, can you erase the scene, completely?

ANDREW: Okay.

(A few minutes later)

MOM: Okay, I want you to picture yourself in your father's study again.

ANDREW: Okay.

MOM: How does it feel?

ANDREW: Well, it's not as bad as before. I'm not totally relaxed, but I feel better. I know that he still cares about me, because he drives a couple of hundred miles every weekend to see me.

MOM: Great.

Andrew's mother repeated the process every few days, until Andrew could picture all of the serious rejections on his list without becoming anxious. Andrew's mother knew that her son would never be totally comfortable with serious rejections. (Nobody is.) But she was able to bring his anxiety about rejection down to a level where it didn't get in the way of more positive thoughts.

A few weeks later, Andrew's mother called to tell me that Andrew had stopped moping around his father's study. When she asked him what had changed, he said, "I'm not as upset as I was. I'm really sad that Daddy's gone, but I know he drives a long way to see me every weekend, so he must love me. And I know he won't forget me."

▼▲

If you're like most parents, you'd love to shield your child from rejection.

You can't.

Rejection is a part of every child's life. And no matter how hard you try to make your child's life comfortable and secure, he's still going to have to live with some rejection.

- The neighbor who moves away.
- The teacher who doesn't call on her the instant she raises her hand.
- The friend who says, "I can't play with you tomorrow. I'm going to spend the day with Susan."
- The classmate who says, "I don't want to sit with you in the cafeteria anymore."
- The parent who decides to have another child.
- The grandparent who dies. (To a very young child, as well as to many adults, death can seem like a form of rejection.)

Here's how your child may be thinking about rejection now:

Scott doesn't want to play with me. I'm not a good friend; I'm not even a good person. I'm worthless. I deserve to be rejected. This is my fault.

Here's how you'd like your child to think about rejection:

Scott doesn't want to play with me. I'm sad about that. Luckily, I have a lot of other friends. I'm a good friend. I'm a worthwhile person. This sort of rejection happens to everyone. It's upsetting, but it's not the end of the world.

You can teach your child to greet mild rejection with the emotional shrug, the shrug that says, "Oh, well. These things happen. I'm upset, but I'll get over it. Lots of people have been rejected before; there's nothing wrong with me because this happened."

Your child can't be made to like—or even shrug off—serious rejection. But she can be taught to cope with it, to feel okay around it ("I've experienced this before, and gotten through it."), to not let it undermine her self-image.

No child is too young to experience rejection. Your child has known rejection practically since birth.

- When you leave his room at night
- When you don't have time to rock her
- When you go off to work

Your child almost certainly feels rejected. By the time he's in school, your child's environment is a minefield of rejection. Friends, classmates, even his teachers may reject him. You can't change that. But you can change the way your child feels about rejection.

Talk about rejection.

Like sex and death, rejection is a subject many parents never bring up.

When was the last time you told your child:

"Mrs. Benson doesn't seem to want to be my friend anymore, and that's hard for me to accept."

"Two of my clients dropped me this week, and it's difficult for me to keep from feeling hurt."

You may want to seem invincible to your child. But you're doing him a disservice if you don't let him know that:

- Rejection happens to everyone (even someone as wonderful as you).
- No one likes rejection. It isn't fun, and it never will be.
- The fear of rejection can be as bad as rejection itself. You can't make friends or form a love relationship if you're overwhelmed by the fear of rejection.
- You can learn not to be devastated by rejection—at least not in its milder forms. When someone says, "I don't want to sit next to you." or "I don't want to play with you."—that doesn't have to ruin your day (or damage your self-image).

Make a point of talking about rejection at least twice a week. Here are the kinds of things you can say:

"I was hoping to be invited to Janice's Christmas party. I wasn't. It hurt for a while, but there are lots of fun things I can do that night."

"I've called the new president of the company three times, and he hasn't called me back once. It's annoying, but I guess he's really busy."

Talk about how *you* handle rejection.

- You realized that it's impossible to be liked by all the people all the time (although you wish you could be).
- You realized that a particular rejection (a small one) wasn't worth feeling terrible about.
- You were able to do an emotional shrug, to say to yourself, "That wasn't fun, but it's certainly not the end of the world."

Let your child know that rejection is never pleasant, but it isn't fatal, either.

If you have specific ways of coping, share them.

PARENT: When a friend doesn't have time to see me, I just think about all the good times we had together when we weren't so busy.

CHILD: I can do the same thing. It makes me feel good to think about the good times I spent with Jenny.

or

PARENT: Whenever I'm feeling lonely, like nobody in the world loves me, I go get those photo albums off the shelf, and I look at them, and I see all the people who care about me, who I've spent time with, and suddenly I feel better.

CHILD: Wow!

PARENT: Maybe we can make you a photo album, and you can have pictures of all your friends there.

CHILD: I think I'd like that.

Encourage your child to talk about rejection.

Children are incredibly embarrassed to talk about rejection— which is something I understand firsthand. When I was nine, my family moved to another neighborhood—and my old friends stopped talking to me; they just shut me out of their lives. And I didn't tell a soul about it—not even my parents. I was too hurt and humiliated.

That's the kind of resistance you're up against in trying to get your child to talk about rejection.

To help draw your child out, you may need to—

Ask questions:

- When was the last time you felt ignored by anyone?
- When was the last time you felt left out?
- When was the last time you felt someone didn't want to be your friend?
- When was the last time you felt someone didn't want to play with you?
- When was the last time you felt someone didn't like you?

You can bring up specific situations:

- How did you feel when Freddy said he was going to the movies with John and didn't invite you?
- How did you feel when Michelle stopped playing with you because she needed more time for horseback riding?
- How did it feel when you ran for class president and lost to someone you don't even like?

Or you can bring up specific emotions (But give your child a choice. You don't want to put words in her mouth!):

- When James said he didn't want to be your friend anymore, did you feel hurt, or upset, or angry?
- When you waited all day for Cynthia to call, and she didn't, were you upset, or mad, or anxious?
- Do you get angry, or disappointed, or sad, when you're one of the last people chosen to play basketball?

Be on the lookout for rejection in unobvious places:

- Perhaps your child feels rejected because you've stopped driving him to school.

- Perhaps he feels rejected by his teacher because he's gotten a low grade.
- Perhaps he feels rejected by his friends because a boy and a girl he introduced have decided to go steady.

Empathize.

CHILD: Sometimes, my teacher doesn't call on me at all, and then the bell rings.
YOU: I understand how unhappy that would make you.

If possible, talk about a similar rejection you once faced, and what you did about it:

YOU: When I was your age, I was really an enthusiastic student, too, and I was always raising my hand. And the teacher couldn't always call on me. So I taught myself to shrug about it. At the end of class, if I hadn't gotten a chance to speak, I'd say to myself, "Well, that wasn't great, but it's okay. I'll get a chance to talk another day." I didn't feel wonderful—I was still a little unhappy—but I did feel better.

Don't minimize your child's feelings.

- Oh, who cares if Steve didn't call you? He's not a very nice person, anyway.
- So what if you didn't get invited to the roller skating party? You can go roller skating anytime.
- You can't really be upset about not getting called on in class, can you? What's the big deal?

You should be reacting to what your child feels—not to what you think he should feel. What seems to you to be a small rejection may be devastating to your child.

Encourage appropriate responses to rejection.

Sally, nine, whose friend didn't invite her to a party:

PARENT: Would you feel better about this if you told Susie you were hurt?

SALLY: I think so.

PARENT: Well if you'd like to, we can talk about what you might say to her. You can even practice saying it to me before you go over to Susie's house and tell her.

Mark, eight, whose best friend moved away:

PARENT: Would you feel better if you wrote him a letter telling him how much you value his friendship?

MARK: Yeah, and then maybe he'll write back, and I'll feel much better.

PARENT: Great. I'll get you some stationery and you can write the letter when you're ready.

Jerry, eleven, whose teacher gave him a bad grade:

PARENT: Would you feel better if we had a meeting with Mrs. Cole to talk about it? Maybe she'll tell you why you got the grade you got, and maybe it has nothing to do with her not liking you.

JERRY: Well, it would be good to find out why she gave me that C.

PARENT: Great, I'll call the school tomorrow and see if we can arrange a time to get together.

Talk about what it's like to be the rejector (as opposed to the rejectee).

James, nine, who was ignored by his best friend:

PARENT: Can you think of a time when you ignored someone you cared about?

JAMES: Yeah, a few weeks ago, I wasn't feeling well, and I didn't pay any attention to Stacy.
PARENT: Well, is it possible that Henry wasn't feeling well today? Maybe that's the reason he ignored you.
JAMES: You're right. I never looked at it that way before.

April, eight, whose friend hasn't returned her phone calls:

PARENT: Can you think of a time when you didn't return someone's call?
APRIL: Yeah. Last week, I was just too busy. So I didn't call Steve back. I figured he would understand.
PARENT: So when Alexis didn't call you back, maybe she was too busy. If someone doesn't call you back, it doesn't necessarily mean she doesn't like you.
APRIL: Yeah, maybe you're right.

Andy, eleven, whose brother says he never wants to talk to him again:

PARENT: I understand you're really hurt because Jack doesn't want to talk to you.
ANDY: Yeah, he obviously doesn't like me.
PARENT: Well, that may not be the reason. Once, when I was a kid, I didn't talk to my brother—your uncle Martin—for weeks. And it wasn't because I didn't like him. I liked him a lot. In fact, I was very jealous of him, and that's why I couldn't face him.
ANDY: Really?
PARENT: Uh-huh. So don't assume that because Jack doesn't want to talk to you, it means he doesn't like you. That may not be the reason.

Deirdre, thirteen, whose date for the school dance canceled at the last minute:

FATHER: It sounds like you're really upset.

DEIRDRE: You're telling me. This is the biggest embarrassment of my life. And I told all my friends he liked me.

FATHER: I hate to say it, but I did the same thing to a girl when I was your age.

DEIRDRE: You did?

FATHER: And it wasn't because I didn't like the girl. I liked her too much. That was the problem. I was extremely nervous.

DEIRDRE: Really?

FATHER: Really. I was too nervous about saying the wrong thing. So don't assume he doesn't like you. Maybe he was just too scared to leave the house.

DEIRDRE: *(Laughing)* Yeah, that does sound like him.

Un-rejections

Like most people, your child probably pays a lot of attention to rejections and takes the love and acceptance he gets—the *un-rejections*—for granted. Rejections hurt his self-image, because he takes them seriously. But un-rejections, which could help his self-image, don't, because he overlooks them.

Ask your child to recall some un-rejections:

- *Rejection:* Martha's mother has decided to take a full-time job.
- *Un-rejection:* She sets aside a lot of time on weekends to be with Martha.

- *Rejection:* Stuart's best friend has just deserted him.
- *Un-rejection:* Lots of other friends are sticking by him.

- *Rejection:* Alison's parents leave her with a babysitter twice a week.
- *Un-rejection:* When they're home, they pay attention to her.

You might ask your child to keep a diary of un-rejections. Or you may just have him tell them to you a few times a week.

PARENT: Tell me about an un-rejection you got today.
CHILD: Well, everyone came over and sat down next to me in the cafeteria.
PARENT: You had lots of company. That was really nice. Anything else?
CHILD: Mrs. Greene called on me a lot.
PARENT: That's great. It sounds like you have a lot to contribute to the class.
CHILD: Yeah, I guess so.

Here are some more un-rejections your child should look for:

- A friend calls.
- She's invited to a party.
- He gets a good grade.
- Someone sits down next to her on the school bus.
- He's chosen for a part in the school play.
- Her grandparents call on her birthday.
- His baby brother wants to play with him.
- Her aunt sends her a present.
- His cousin comes over to play.
- She gets asked back to a friend's house for dinner.

For writing down (or remembering) un-rejections, you may want to reward your child with points. ("When you have ten points, we'll go out to that ice-cream place you like so much.")

Make a hierarchy.

Rank rejections on a scale of one (least disturbing; easily shrugged off) to ten (most disturbing; the worst your child can imagine).

With a young child, you may have to create the hierarchy yourself (assigning numbers on the basis of how your child feels about each situation). An older child can assign her own numbers.

Either way, the simple act of "ranking" rejections will reduce your child's anxiety. Saying, "I think it's an eight or a nine." is far less traumatic than saying, "I feel awful." Using numbers enables your child to be objective about some very upsetting emotions.

Include anticipatory (imagined) rejections.

Many children are so exquisitely sensitive to rejection that they worry about rejections that haven't happened and probably never will. To your child, anticipatory rejections can be very real, and very scary. During one of your discussions, ask your child if there are any rejections he worries about that haven't happened. If he says yes, don't scoff ("But that'll never happen. Don't be silly.") Instead, be empathetic ("I can see how that would scare you."). The important thing is to deal with your child's feelings, whatever they may be.

SEYMOUR'S HIERARCHY

Age: five

Biggest problem: Has a hard time making friends.

1. My cat won't come over to be petted; she'd rather go outside.
2. My teacher called on Bobby, not me, and I had my hand raised.

3. My mother kept on talking to my older sister, even though I had something important to say.

4. My father kept watching the movie on TV, after I told him I wanted to speak to him.

5. When the kids chose up sides for baseball, I was picked fourth and Bobby was picked first.

6. Don's mom took him and two other kids into town, and they didn't ask me to go along.

7. The soccer coach didn't notice that I was out three days last week.

8. Johnny and Brian played together after school, and they didn't ask me to join them.

9. Grandma came over and spent the whole time playing with my little sister.

10. (Anticipatory) Don says he doesn't want to be my friend anymore.

JANE'S HIERARCHY

Age: nine

Biggest problem: She's about to move to another city, and she's terrified she won't make friends there.

1. She calls her friend Lois and leaves a message, but doesn't hear back for three days.

2. Some of her friends lose interest in her because she's moving away, and they don't talk to her.

3. Her brother says she's creepy and he doesn't want to speak to her ever again.

4. (Anticipatory) Her brother tells her friends bad things about her, and they stop talking to her.

5. (Anticipatory) The people in her new city don't like her.

6. (Anticipatory) Her mother and father have a bad fight, and her father storms out of the house.

7. (Anticipatory) The day she arrives at her new school, no one is friendly to her.

8. (Anticipatory) She's been in her new school for two months, and she still doesn't have any friends.

9. (Anticipatory) She goes back to her old school, and no one recognizes her.

10. (Anticipatory) Her parents say they're going to move, but she has to stay where she is.

Using the hierarchy

For items 1–5:

Begin teaching your child the emotional shrug.

YOU: You're feeling hurt and rejected because Brian didn't invite you to his house to play. I know how bad that can make you feel. But there are things you can do to make yourself feel better.

CHILD: What?

YOU: First, you can admit to yourself how hurt you feel. That's normal and human. Do you understand that everyone faces rejection, and everyone feels awful when it happens?

CHILD: Yes.

YOU: Good. Then maybe you can tell yourself that you can play with another friend instead. I know how much you like Brian. But say to yourself, "As much as I miss him, there are other people I like to play with, too."

CHILD: There *are* other people.

YOU: Good. This is an upsetting thing, but it's not the end of the world. Can you try saying that?

CHILD: This isn't the end of the world. I'm upset, but I'll live.

YOU: Great. I know this is difficult. I know how hurt you are by the situation. But you're doing really well. I want you to think about what happened with Brian, and I want you to shrug to yourself. It's not that you don't miss Brian, it's just that you'll get over this.

(Child shrugs)

YOU: What were you thinking?

CHILD: That as much as I miss him, I'll get over it. I'll live.

YOU: I think you're getting the idea.

Work on the emotional shrug five times a week for two weeks. It may seem like an awkward exercise at first, but it will soon be second nature.

Have your child begin using the emotional shrug in the "real world," and keep an eye on how he's doing. Ask him to tell you about the rejections he faces, and how he reacts. You may want to reward him each time he responds correctly.

For items 6–10:

These are the serious rejections, the ones your child can't shrug off. You can reason with him, and let him know that he hasn't been singled out—that the rejection that's upsetting him so much may in fact have nothing to do with him. And you can get him to think about un-rejections. But before you can do those things, you'll need to reduce his anxiety—anxiety that makes it hard for him to "just listen to reason."

When someone teases or criticizes your child, he can confront that person. And that helps him feel assertive (instead of simply hurt or anxious). Assertiveness crowds out the anxiety your child would otherwise feel. With most rejections, though, there's no way your child can confront the person who upset him. (The rejector may have died, or moved away, or stopped talking to her completely.) Instead, you'll have to take steps to reduce your child's anxiety using relaxation techniques. Once you do, he'll be able to deal more rationally with his situation.

To relax your child, you can:

- Have him lie down in a comfortable place.
- Let her hold a favorite doll or stuffed animal.
- Turn the lights down low.
- Play soothing music.
- Have him close his eyes.
- Ask him to say the word *calm* to himself, slowly, each time he exhales.

or

- Have her picture her body becoming as limp as a wet noodle.

or

- Have him picture himself becoming as relaxed as a sleeping kitten.

or

- Have her focus on an imaginary scoop of melting ice cream.

or

- Have him tense a part of his body, then release it and focus on how relaxed it has become.

YOU: I want you to think about your forehead. First wrinkle it to tense it. Then frown to tense it even more. Now relax it. Now it's totally relaxed, totally smooth. It has no lines, no wrinkles.
CHILD: Okay.
YOU: Good. Keep thinking about it. Just picture how smooth and unwrinkled it is . . .

After a few minutes, ask your child to picture the rejection that upset him. Ask him if he feels upset. If he says yes, have him erase the scene. Then repeat whichever relaxation technique works best for him. When your child tells you he's relaxed, have him picture the rejection scene again.

Repeat these steps until your child tells you he's completely relaxed while imagining the rejection.

Now that he's relaxed, you can begin to use reason to lessen his discomfort. Tell him about the flip side of the rejection (the un-rejection). Tell him that the rejection doesn't make him a bad person. Tell him that the rejection may not have anything to do with him.

"I know Marla said she wouldn't go out on a date with you [rejection]. But three other girls said they would [un-rejection]. I want you to think about those other girls for as long as you like."

Because your child has calmed down, he'll be able to focus on your message—perhaps for the first time. Once you've gotten your message across, have your child erase the scene again. After a few minutes, have him picture the scene one last time. Ask him how he feels. Chances are your child won't be nearly as anxious as before. Ask him what he's thinking and what he's seeing. He should be able to remember some of the things you said to help him cope with the rejection.

"Well, there are three other girls who want to go out with me, so why should I be so upset about Marla?"

Congratulate him on learning to relax in the face of serious rejection.

SUMMARY

Talk about rejection, at least twice a week. Talk about times you faced rejection, and about how you coped.

Encourage your child to talk about rejection. Use patience, positive reinforcement, and empathy to help him open up.

Empathize. (Tell your child you understand what he's feeling).

Encourage appropriate responses to rejection. ("Why not write her a letter and tell her how you feel?")

Help your child think about un-rejections (the people who like her, who visit her, who call her).

Gradually use the information your child gives you to form a rejection hierarchy, from one (mild) to ten (terribly painful).

For the mild rejections (1–5): Teach your child the emotional shrug—the feeling of "This isn't great, but I can live with it. This happens to everyone, and it isn't the end of the world." Have your child report back on rejections he faces and how he responds. Praise or reward him for using the emotional shrug.

For severe rejections (6–10): Teach your child to replace rejections in her mind with un-rejections.

But before you can do that, you may have to turn down the "temperature" of her emotions, using the relaxation techniques on page 176.

9

▮▮

THE BODY-IMAGE
TRIP

AUDREY'S STORY

In a society that idolizes perfect-looking people, Audrey, age twelve, wasn't perfect, and she knew it.

If you asked her about her looks, she'd tell you that:

- Her breasts weren't large enough.
- Her hair wasn't shiny enough.
- Her legs weren't long enough.
- Her skin wasn't clear enough.
- Her eyes weren't big enough.

In fact, there was nothing wrong with Audrey's looks. But in her mind, her liabilities seemed vast; her assets, tiny. Like many adolescents, Audrey was scared about becoming a grownup, and being unsure of her looks made the transition that much harder. The way Audrey imagined it, there was a sign at the entrance to the adult world: UNATTRACTIVE GIRLS NEED NOT APPLY. Audrey was barely on the verge of adulthood, but she already felt shut out.

Audrey's mother had an idea what her daughter was going through. As a child, Audrey's mother hadn't been unattractive— just average-looking. But average was bad enough. Audrey's mother remembered the pain she had endured when she was Audrey's age, and she wanted to make things easier for Audrey. She wanted Audrey to recognize the parts of her that *were* attractive. She wanted Audrey to realize that in order to look good, she didn't have to look like Christie Brinkley.

But Audrey's mother didn't know how to do that. Just talking to Audrey about her appearance was difficult. Whenever her mother mentioned looks, Audrey would walk away or change the subject.

Audrey's parents thought it might help to compliment her appearance, and a few times Audrey's father told her she was gorgeous. But she wasn't gorgeous, and she knew it.

Not knowing how to help their daughter made Audrey's parents feel like they were letting her down.

Luckily, Audrey's school ran a series of seminars for parents. One night I spoke about the importance of body image to adolescents. It's difficult, I said, for any teenager to have a positive self-image unless she's comfortable with her appearance. Then I outlined an eight-step program for helping kids "get along with their looks." Audrey's parents were at the seminar. They took notes, and the next morning they told Audrey that they had found a way to help her feel more comfortable with her appearance. Just hearing that made Audrey incredibly anxious. But when Audrey's parents told her that what they were going to do was in the form of a game, she began to relax.

Step One:
Audrey's parents asked her to think about some of her favorite people, and to list the things she liked about them. Here are some of her responses.

Mrs. Kimble (teacher):
Encourages students
Cares about people's problems
Has a great sense of humor

Janice (friend):
Loyal
Makes time for Audrey
Intelligent

Mother:
Patient and thoughtful
Successful at career
Talented

Looks weren't on any of her lists. When her parents mentioned that, Audrey said, "Looks are just looks; that's not why you like somebody."
Said her mother, "Exactly."
The next day, when Audrey was reading the newspaper, her father asked her to make a list of people she admired. Audrey's list included

- Mario Cuomo (her governor)
- Margaret Thatcher
- Ralph Nader
- Roseanne Barr (the star of her favorite TV show).

Audrey realized there was no one gorgeous on her list. Indeed, when her father said, "But Roseanne's so overweight," Audrey answered, "Yeah, but that doesn't mean I can't like her."
Said her father, "Exactly."

Step Two:

The next day, Audrey's mother asked her to spend ten minutes thinking about some of the things she liked about her looks. Audrey thought, *But I don't like anything.*

"You may not think there's anything to like," said Audrey's mother, practically reading Audrey's mind. "But you're wrong. And if you spend ten minutes working your way down from head to toe, making a lot of stops along the way, I think you'll start to see that."

Audrey agreed to try—to take a silent body-image trip. Her mother asked her to start at the top of her head, and then to slowly work her way down to her face, her neck, her shoulders. "Along the way," Audrey's mother said, "you should stop for a while and think about the things you like. If you get to something you don't like, don't worry about it. Go back to something you like. Think about *that* until you feel better, and then go on." To further encourage Audrey, she said, "I'll help you get going. Okay? Let's start with your hair. Is there anything you like about that?" Audrey thought to herself that her hair did feel silky and wonderful. She smiled, and her mother let her stay with that thought for a minute.

Then her mother said, "How about your eyes? Do you like anything about your eyes?" *They're a pretty nice color,* Audrey thought to herself.

"How about your nose?" Audrey didn't much like her nose. Instead, she went right back to thinking (happily) about the color of her eyes.

Eventually Audrey's mother asked her about her lips, her tongue, her teeth, her chin, her neck, the shape of her face, even the sound of her laugh. She encouraged Audrey to think about the features she liked (to Audrey's surprise, there were many more than she'd realized!), and to ignore the ones she disliked.

Audrey's mother didn't ask Audrey to *say* anything. She just wanted her to *think* about her many likable features.

Step Three:

The next day, Audrey's mother asked her to talk about *one* of the things she liked about herself.

Audrey said she would try.

To encourage her, her mother said, "I'll do it, too."

And then Audrey's mother said, "I like the way my hair feels. Now you tell me something you like about *your* appearance."

Audrey answered, "My hair feels terrific, too."

Every day for a week, Audrey and her mother traded things they liked about their looks. Here are some of their exchanges.

MOTHER: I like the size of my eyes.
AUDREY: I like the color of my eyes.

MOTHER: I like how strong my legs feel when I run.
AUDREY: I like how strong my arms feel when I play tennis.

When Audrey couldn't come up with an answer, her mother asked her questions:

- Do you like your new haircut?
- Do you like the way your hair smells after it's been washed?
- Do you like the way your hair falls into place?
- Do you like the shape of your eyes?
- Do you like the dimple in your chin when you smile?
- Do you like the whiteness of your teeth?

(On the trip from head to toe, Audrey's mother skipped *anything a bathing suit would cover.* The "bathing suit rule" is a way of making sure that no one is embarrassed.)

Step Four:

Already, Audrey was seeing "self-positives" that had eluded her for years. To help her along, her parents complimented her appearance every day.

Here are some of the things they told her:

- You have such a great smile.
- You have a wonderfully slim figure.
- Your legs look so powerful when you run.
- Your complexion is so clear.

Naturally they stayed away from hyperbole ("You're the prettiest girl in the school"). And they never once said, "You have such an interesting face." Audrey—like everyone else—knew "interesting" to be a euphemism for "not pretty."

Whenever they complimented her, Audrey's parents paid attention to how Audrey responded. If she looked embarrassed, or walked away, or didn't answer, they encouraged her to say, "Thank you, it's so nice of you to notice," in a firm voice, and to use assertive body language (to stand or sit up straight, with heart held high). When she did these things, they gave her positive reinforcement. ("You're getting so much better at accepting compliments about your looks, Audrey. Terrific!")

Step Five:

Audrey was becoming so good at talking about her looks that her parents felt she was ready for the next step: taking a body-image trip *aloud*.

Audrey asked her mother, "Why aloud, when it's so much easier to say it to myself?" .

"This way, if you're having any problems, I'll be able to help you," said her mother. Audrey's mother made the body-image trip into a game. "The idea," she said, "is to exchange attractive features. I'll go first, and then you go, and then I'll go, and so on." Then she started at the top of her head. "I love the way my hair feels after I wash it," said Audrey's mother. "Now it's your turn."

"I think my hair looks really nice when it's combed like this," said Audrey.

"Good," said Audrey's mother. "Now I'll do another one. I like the smoothness of my forehead. Now you give me one."

Answered Audrey, "I think I have a nice forehead, too."

In ten minutes they worked their way down to the floor (still observing the bathing suit rule), happily exchanging things they liked about their looks.

The next day, Audrey's mother taped a sign to the mirror in Audrey's room. The sign said, THERE ARE SO MANY THINGS TO LIKE ABOUT YOURSELF. Audrey said she was going to leave that message there forever.

Step Six:

Audrey and her mother took a body-image trip each week. Sometimes Audrey repeated things she'd said before, but she also came up with lots of new ones. To her surprise, her list of likable features was still growing.

Step Seven:

Audrey's mother asked Audrey if anyone ever complimented her about her looks.

"No, not really," said Audrey.

"Are you sure?" asked her mother.

Audrey shrugged.

"Just in case," said her mother, "I'd like you to take a piece of paper, and whenever anyone says something nice about your appearance, write it down."

Audrey agreed.

In the next two weeks, Audrey wrote down more than twenty compliments, including these:

- From her father: You look beautiful in that dress.
- From her friend Suzanne: I wish I had blond hair like yours; it's gorgeous.
- From her grandmother: You're as pretty as your Aunt Irene was when she was your age. And your Aunt Irene was so popular with the boys.

As her list grew longer, Audrey began to realize that a lot of people had a lot of nice things to say about her looks. Keeping a journal forced her to pay attention to the compliments she had been receiving all along but had somehow failed to notice.

Step Eight:
By now, Audrey was receiving compliments about her appearance every day. (What she was finding out is that if you accept compliments gracefully, they keep coming!) Her father felt she was ready to talk about a few of her faults in a new, positive light. Audrey's father asked her to think about something she didn't like about her looks, and then say something kind about it. To show her what to do, he demonstrated:

"Well, I'm partly bald, but so what? Some of the sexiest actors in Hollywood are bald. Sure, I don't have the greatest nose in the world. But I'm used to it, and I think it's kind of cute."

"It is kind of cute, Daddy," said Audrey.

Then Audrey's father asked Audrey to talk about her appearance in the same way. "Okay, Audrey, now you try."

"Well, my hair gets all kinky when it rains, but so what? I'll just have to move to the desert when I grow up."

Then they both laughed. A few months ago, Audrey would

have cried thinking about her hair. Now she was joking about it. It was okay for her to joke, because by now she knew she had a lot of good points. And in that context, her few small imperfections really didn't matter.

By the time they completed the eighth step, Audrey's parents were thrilled with the changes they were seeing in their daughter. Audrey seemed more confident, more self-assured. She had an easier time buying clothes and she was becoming a regular at junior-high-school dances, which she had previously been afraid to attend.

Audrey's parents wanted her new attitude to last. So they began incorporating bits of the eight steps into their everyday routine.

As often as they could, they complimented some aspect of her appearance. If she thanked them "properly," they complimented her again.

Some days they would also ask Audrey to "Tell me something you like about your looks." If she couldn't think of anything to say, they made suggestions ("How do you feel about the way you look in that new sweater? Don't you like how nice your teeth look after that visit to the dentist?").

They would talk about people they liked (or admired) who weren't especially attractive, or who were attractive in an unusual way.

They would exchange "I like my . . ." statements. First Audrey's mother would say, "I like how smooth my legs feel after I shave them," and Audrey would say, "Yeah, my legs feel great, too," and so on.

Once in a while, Audrey and her mother took a full-fledged body-image trip together.

And every time they could, they would joke about their imperfections. For the first time ever, Audrey's imperfections didn't loom large in her mind. In fact, they were starting to seem pretty minor.

By now, Audrey seemed to have made peace with her looks. She knew she wasn't Christie Brinkley. She didn't need to be. There were a lot of things to like about *Audrey's* appearance. She liked them and, to her amazement, a lot of other people liked them, too.

She would never be the most gorgeous girl in her class. But the most gorgeous girl in her class might not have been as secure about her looks as Audrey had become.

Her parents had given her a terrific present: not a new way to look, but something even better: a new way of looking at herself.

A note about your daughter

Since infancy, your daughter has known that looks do matter ("Oh, you'll be as beautiful as your mother someday.")—and the pressure that puts on her can be overwhelming. What's more, the attention our society pays to women's hair, makeup, and clothing has sent her a message: her natural appearance isn't good enough; she has to struggle to "improve" it. The fact that anorexia and bulimia occur almost exclusively in girls is one indication of the pressure girls can feel to make themselves look "better." By the time she was seven or eight, your daughter may have been asking herself, "Why aren't I as pretty as that girl?" "Will anyone like me if I stay this fat?" "How can I get blue eyes like hers." In adolescence, the questions may become even more pressing: "When are my breasts going to develop?" "Why aren't they bigger?" "Will these pimples ever go away?" "Is this much hair on my legs normal?" "Will boys find me attractive?" As a parent, you may want to help your daughter "relax" about her looks, using the techniques in this chapter.

A note about your son

Body image can be as much of an issue for boys as for girls—although they worry about different things. In our society, boys feel they have to be tall, and strong, and handsome. Your son may make it to adolescence without worrying much about his looks—but in adolescence, that's likely to change. He may find himself asking questions like, "When will I have hair on my chest?" "Will these pimples stay with me forever?" "Will I ever have to shave?" "I'm only five three—will I grow another twelve inches? Okay, God, how about another *six* inches?" "Are the other boys in the locker room using steroids, or are they just working out more?" "I work out—why don't I look as good as them?" And, of course, the sixty-four-thousand-dollar question: "Is my penis big enough?" As a parent, you may want to help your son "relax" about his looks, using the techniques in this chapter.

The link between body-image and overall self-image is a strong one. In our society, we associate physical beauty with strength, intelligence, and virtue. So it's not surprising that a child who sees herself as unattractive may also have a weak self-image. It's practically impossible for a child to feel good about herself if she's uncomfortable with her appearance.

But you can't convince your child that she's gorgeous if she isn't, nor would you want to (self-delusion is never the basis of a good self-image). What you can do is change the way she sees herself, so that her few flaws no longer outweigh her many strengths in her mind.

Does your child have a body-image problem?

- If she refuses to buy clothes until she loses another ten pounds
- If he doesn't want to go to the beach, because he thinks he's too skinny
- If she doesn't want to go to a party (because she's ashamed of her complexion)
- If he spends hours staring at himself in the mirror
- If she refuses to eat more than a salad
- If he talks about taking steroids
- If she spends a fortune on beauty products
- If he's afraid that girls won't like him
- If she won't go to a school dance, because she thinks no one will talk to her

the answer is probably "yes."

But my daughter is gorgeous!

Don't think that because your child is good-looking, she can't possibly have a body-image problem. In my work with children, I've found that being gorgeous is no guarantee of a good self-image. (Indeed, the correlation between attractiveness and self-esteem is vague or nonexistent.) I have counseled world-famous models who couldn't come up with a single answer to the question, "Tell me something you like about the way you look."

Even if your child *is* gorgeous, the memory of a time when she was heavy, awkward, or unattractive may be fixed in her mind. What's important isn't how she looks on the outside—but how her looks *feel* on the inside.

What's more, if your child doesn't think of herself as attractive, nothing she does to "improve" her looks will change that. Your child can eat less, exercise more, get contact lenses, have her teeth straightened, her nose fixed (and maybe some of those things are a good idea)—but none of them can guarantee a good self-image.

Luckily, a feeling of contentment with her looks is far more attractive than any physical characteristic. And you can help her attain that contentment by using the techniques in this chapter.

In improving your child's body image, you have some powerful enemies:

■ Mass media (including TV, movies, and magazines), with their barrage of images of perfect-looking people. (No matter how self-confident she is, it's hard for your child to avoid comparing herself to movie stars and models.)
■ Friends and peers, who magically decide what's in and what's out, what looks right and what doesn't. (No child, no matter how strong her self-image, is entirely immune to this pressure.)

You can't eliminate these powerful forces, but you can cushion their impact on your child. You can give him tools to use throughout his life, whenever he feels less than comfortable with his appearance.

Audrey's parents rarely spent more than ten minutes a day on their "body-image project." Yet they began seeing dramatic changes in their daughter's attitude in just two weeks. By working together, they were able to give each other reinforcement and relief.

The techniques can be carried out by two parents together, or two parents taking turns, or by one parent (in a one- or two-parent household).* However you do them, they are meant to be treated as a game, with high spirits and humor.

You don't have to attempt all eight steps, or even seven, or six. (Audrey's parents did all eight steps in order, but you don't have to.) Pick and choose from the list, and skip any technique that makes your child anxious.

Step One:

Talk about people you like who aren't gorgeous. Discuss how insignificant their physical "flaws" really are compared to the things you like about them. If you can, identify some famous people with the same "flaws" as your child (a bucktoothed movie star, a singer with frizzy hair). The idea is to show your child that less-than-perfect looks are no bar to personal and professional success. Some of my favorites are Danny DeVito, Bob Dylan, and Barbara Bush. None of them would have won third prize in a beauty contest, but all of them command the attention of millions.

CHILD: Oh, yeah, Danny DeVito is shorter than me, but he's one of the biggest stars in Hollywood.
PARENT: That's right. Whoever said you have to be tall to be successful?

You should also help your child identify a few people around her who are less than perfect looking—but who are otherwise terrific.

---

*In most families, the techniques in this chapter are best left to the same-sex parent (or friend or other family member). However, there's no reason why the other parent can't help out (for instance, by complimenting the child's appearance, or by helping her think of famous people who are less-than-perfect looking).

"Martha's really nice. I like her a lot. She's a little overweight, but that doesn't matter."

By acknowledging that she doesn't judge people on the basis of their looks, your child will begin to understand that other people don't judge her on the basis of her looks.

Step Two:

Ask your child to take a silent body-image trip. Starting at the top of her head, have her work her way down, slowly, to her forehead, her nose, her ears, her mouth—all the way down to her toes. Along the way, have her identify everything she likes, no matter how minute. She should be encouraged to include the feel of things ("My hands feel smooth." "My legs help me run fast.") as well as their outward appearance. Along the way, your child should push away negative thoughts, skipping over any parts of her body that she doesn't find attractive. (She's spent enough time dwelling on those already.)

If you need to, help your child by asking questions:

- Is there anything you like about your hair?
- How do you feel about your eyes?
- What do you think of the shape of your mouth?
- Is there anything you like about your nose, lips, tongue, chin, neck, the sound of your laugh?

Remember: This step should be done silently; you want your child to become comfortable with the idea of the body-image trip. Encourage him to think about his favorite parts, but don't make him talk about them—yet.

Step Three:

Each day, ask your child to tell you several things she likes about her looks. If she has trouble *discussing* her looks with you, have her write down her answers. Then, gradually, encourage her to talk about them.

To reassure your child, you may want to play the trading game:

"I'll tell you something I like about myself; then you tell me something you like about yourself. Okay?"

For a girl:

"I love the way my legs feel when I put on stockings. Now you tell me something you like."

For a boy:

"I love how smooth my face feels after I shave. Now you tell me something you like."

And you may want to ask questions. Ask about small things— *things you know your child likes.*

- Do you like the way your hair smells when you wash it?
- Do you like the way your hair shines?
- Do you remember what Joyce said about your new haircut?
- Do you like the way your hair falls into place?
- Do you like the color of your eyes?
- Do you like the sparkle in your eyes?
- Do you like your smile?
- Do you remember what Aunt Dorothy said about your smile?
- Do you like how strong your legs feel when you run?
- Do you like how strong your arms feel when you swim?

Don't ask questions your child can't possibly say yes to:

"Don't you think you're gorgeous?"
"Don't you realize that you're the prettiest girl (handsomest boy) in your class?"

If your child answers "no" to one of your questions, don't panic. Say something like, "Well, that's okay. You can't like everything. Let's look for some things you *do* like."

Step Four:
Compliment your child's appearance every day. Make the compliments believable (by making them specific):

Not "You're beautiful," *but* "I love how your eyes crinkle up when you smile."
Not "You're the prettiest girl I know," *but* "I want to tell you how much I like your new haircut."
Not "You're the handsomest boy I know," *but* "You look very mature in that suit."

Make your compliments honest. Don't try to fool your child by picking out her worst feature and telling her how much you like it. Children have a talent for spotting deception.

Encourage your child to respond

■ by saying "Thank you" in a firm voice
■ by making eye contact
■ by standing or sitting up straight (with heart held high)

If your child does those things correctly, tell him so:

"Wonderful. You accepted that compliment just right."

If she still doesn't feel comfortable receiving compliments ("You're just saying that because I'm your daughter; it isn't true."), use role reversal to demonstrate the desired behavior. ("Okay, I'll be you. Give me a compliment, and I'll show you how I accept it . . .")

Step Five:

Ask your child to take a body-image trip aloud. (Starting at the top of her head, have her work her way down to her toes, describing everything she likes along the way.)

Why have your child take a body-image trip aloud if it's easier for her to do it silently?

- She needs to find out that there's nothing silly or embarrassing about being comfortable with her appearance. The way for her to learn that is to talk about her looks aloud—and for you to praise her as she does it.
- If your child isn't finding enough things about himself to praise, you'll find out, and you'll have an opportunity to help him. ("How about your arms? They're so much stronger now that you've been swimming.")

To avoid embarrassment, remember to skip over anything a bathing suit would cover.

When your child gets to the end of her body-image trip, add a few more compliments. The idea is to show her that the list of things to like about herself is endless.

Step Six:

Repeat step 5 twice a week for two weeks.

To show your child that you feel comfortable with what you're doing, take a body-image trip with her. Make the joint body-image trip a game. "Okay, I'll go first, then you go. We'll take turns, and we'll see who can come up with the most good things. Okay?" Encourage—but don't one-up—your child.

Step Seven:

Ask your child to write down any compliments she gets about her looks. You may want to reward her for writing down ten, or twenty, or fifty compliments, and for accepting them "correctly." The object isn't for your child to fish for compliments, but to be more *aware* of the compliments she's already getting.

Step Eight:

Ask your child to show her appearance a little kindness to make up for the harsh criticism she has given it in the past.

Specifically: Ask her to talk about her physical "flaws" in a lighthearted way. Tell her to be gentle to her imperfections and to laugh about them. If your child can handle this step, she has become genuinely relaxed about her appearance.

When you've completed all eight steps, don't stop. Work the ones you like the best into your everyday routine. In that way you'll be able to help your child build on her successes.

SUMMARY

Use as many of the eight steps as you can, without doing anything to make your child uncomfortable.

(Steps 2–6 are most easily handled by the same-sex parent.)

1. Talk about people you like who aren't gorgeous.

2. Ask your child to take a silent body-image trip, identifying (to herself) at least a dozen things she likes about her looks.

3. Have your child tell you at least one thing he likes about his appearance.

4. Compliment some aspect of your child's appearance every day. Start with something small and believable, not "You're gorgeous."

5. Have your child take a body-image trip aloud, identifying everything she likes about herself, from head to toe. To encourage her, take at least one "trip" with her.

6. Repeat step 5 twice a week for two weeks.

7. Have your child keep a record of compliments she receives about her looks—and her responses.

8. Encourage your child to talk good-naturedly about his imperfections.

10

██▄▄██

THE IMPORTANCE OF
BEING IMPERFECT

JAMIE'S STORY

Though she was one of the smartest seventh-graders in her school, Jamie, thirteen, was so hung up on getting A's, and so intent on always being right, that her teachers (and many of her classmates) found her difficult to be with.

In class, if she thought she knew the answer to a question, she would demand to be called on, sometimes cutting off other students in the rush to demonstrate her superior knowledge. If she didn't know an answer, she would refuse to say anything, declining (in no uncertain terms) to "take a guess" or "estimate." (The possibility of being wrong scared her.) She put all her effort into homework assignments that got graded, disregarding less "important" (but equally interesting) projects. She didn't work well with her classmates, who sometimes found her obnoxious. Not surprisingly, she often seemed lonely.

As I later learned, Jamie had demanding, high-achieving parents who complained when she got less than perfect grades. What's more, she had three older brothers, all of whom had been excellent students. Some of her teachers expected her to be "as good as they were," and when she wasn't, she became distraught.

One of Jamie's teachers referred her to the school counselor, who in turn asked me if I could help her. At our first meeting, Jamie had a hard time admitting anything was wrong. When I asked her about school, she said, "Oh, I guess I just need to study harder," ignoring what was really happening. (If anything, she was studying too much—and enjoying too little.)

I asked her to tell me about something she had done well that day, and she couldn't think of anything. But when I asked her to tell me about something she had done badly, she was quick to answer: she had forgotten to do her arithmetic homework, and her teacher had criticized her for it.

"What about your other subjects?" I asked her.

"Oh, nothing special happened today."

I tried again. "Is there anything you feel you did well today?"
(Silence)

"Did you get any other grades today?"

"Oh, yeah, I got one hundred on the spelling test. And my teacher said I could represent the school in the county spelling bee."

"That's great, Jamie. Why didn't you tell me about that before?"

"I don't know. I just didn't think of it."

A few days later I met with Jamie's parents. Fastidious, well-organized, professional, Jamie's father seemed to want to run his family like a business. During a fifty-minute meeting, he sat stiffly, never unbuttoning his jacket. His curt answers made it clear that he wasn't used to spending time on "family problems." I asked him about Jamie's schoolwork. He told me that on her last report card, she had gotten three A's and two B's, and that upset him. "I got all A's, and I'm sure my wife did, too," he said. "There's no reason for Jamie to get B's."

Jamie's mother was less forbidding than her husband, but she, too, wanted everything to be just right. She, too, had complained about the B's on Jamie's last report card. "All of my boys were top students," she said. "If Jamie weren't as bright, I would make allowances. But I can tell she's just as smart as any of my sons."

I suggested to Jamie's parents that they might be putting too much pressure on her to be perfect. Though they didn't say they agreed with me, they did say they would continue working with me if I thought I could help Jamie.

At my next meeting with Jamie and her parents, I asked Jamie why grades were so important to her. She didn't answer, so I switched to a less "open-ended" question: "How did you feel about your last report card."

JAMIE: Angry.

ME: Angry? Why?

JAMIE: Because the last time we got report cards, one girl in my school said she was going to get five dollars for every A she brought home, and another girl said she was going to get ten dollars. I knew I wouldn't get anything for my A's, and I would get yelled at for my B's. It isn't fair.

Jamie's mother interrupted. "But those girls aren't as smart as you, Jamie. Their parents need to reward them so they can get A's. You can get A's easily. We shouldn't have to bribe you."

"What do you think about that?" I asked Jamie. "Do you want your mother to pay you for getting A's?"

"No," she said, "but I'd like her to at least notice them."

"Doesn't she notice them?" I asked.

"Not really," said Jamie. "She pays attention to everything I do wrong, but she doesn't notice anything I do right."

"Do your parents ever do anything wrong?" I asked her.

She looked dumbfounded by my question.

"What do you think?" I asked her. "Are your parents perfect?"

Gradually Jamie answered, "Well, they act like they are. But I don't think anybody's perfect."

"Do you feel like you're perfect?" I asked Jamie's parents.

"Hardly," said Jamie's father. "In my business, I make mistakes all the time. The trick is to try to succeed more than you fail, but you fail a lot."

Here's how the conversation continued:

ME: Do you ever talk to Jamie about your failures?

DAD: What would be the point of that? I mean, a father is supposed to be a role model, isn't he?

ME: Yes, but, as Jamie said, nobody's perfect.

DAD: Well, I don't know if I feel comfortable talking about my mistakes, even if I do make them.

ME: It's uncomfortable for anyone to talk about making mistakes. But not being perfect is one of the things that makes us human.

DAD: I guess you're right. There's no reason for me to pretend I'm perfect.

JAMIE: (To me) This is the first time I've ever heard him say he isn't perfect. I can't believe he fails at things but never said so. Why?

ME: Your parents probably want you to respect them and look up to them. That's why they can't tell you about the things they do wrong. It's scary for them to admit they sometimes fail. (To Jamie's parents) Isn't that it?

MOM: Well, yes.

ME: Jamie, is it important to you that your parents be perfect?

JAMIE: No way. It's easier for me to love them when they aren't.

At our next meeting, I asked each member of the family to "tell me something you did that you felt good about today."

JAMIE: I can't think of anything.

MOM: Well, I signed up a new client today, after three months of meetings, so that felt terrific.

ME: That's great. Anyone else?

DAD: I had to talk to an employee who wasn't working out, and I like the way I handled it.

ME: That's really nice to hear.

ME: Jamie, you see, it doesn't have to be anything big. Just a small thing you did well. Was there anything?

(*Jamie is silent*)

ME: Can anyone help her out by suggesting something?

MOM: How about the way you helped Jim next door with his times tables?

JAMIE: Yeah, I guess that was pretty good.

MOM: It was. I was very proud of you. You should have seen her, dear.

DAD: I wish I had. It sounds like you were really helpful.

ME: Now I want to ask all of you another question. Was there something you *didn't* do well today?

(*Silence all around*)

ME: Were you all perfect today?

MOM: Okay, I got lost on the way to a meeting, and I ended up getting there late. I was terribly embarrassed.

DAD: It sounds like you felt awful. But remember, you landed a new client today. Besides, everyone's been late for meetings; it's no big deal.

MOM: Thanks. I'm glad you feel that way.

ME: That's great. You helped your wife put her mistake in perspective. That was just the right thing to do. Anyone else?

DAD: I left an important report on my night table, so I didn't have it when I needed it at work.

MOM: Well, I know how difficult that made things for you, but think about all the things you did right today.

ME: Great. You're acknowledging that there's nothing so terrible about making a mistake. Jamie, how do you feel about the conversation your parents just had?

JAMIE: Pretty good. It's nice to know they understand what it's like to mess up.

Before Jamie's parents left, I asked them to spend a minute or two each day talking to Jamie about their mistakes. I asked them to be open with her about their failures and imperfections.

At our next session, they told me about some of the mistakes they had discussed with Jamie.

DAD: Well, I had a fender-bender this week. I have to admit it was my fault. I misjudged a turn. I banged my car up pretty good, but no one was hurt.

ME: Jamie, how did that make you feel?

JAMIE: Well, I just told him I still love him, and it was just an accident.

ME: I'm glad to hear that. How do you think your parents feel when you make a mistake?

JAMIE: I don't know.

ME: Don't you think they feel the same way you do?

(Jamie is silent)

ME: *(To Jamie's parents)* Do you want Jamie to know that it's okay for her to make a mistake?

DAD: I guess so.

ME: Why don't you tell her how you feel when she makes a mistake.

DAD: The same way she does when I make a mistake. I don't love her any less because of a mistake. How could I?

ME: Can you tell *her* that?

DAD: Sure. Jamie, I don't love you any less because of a mistake. I can't believe you didn't know that.

JAMIE: Well, you never told me that before.

DAD: You're right.

ME: Jamie, can you tell us about something you did wrong.

JAMIE: Well, I read the wrong book for a book report, by accident, and now I'm really in trouble with Mrs. Levine.

ME: *(To Jamie's mother)* How did that make you feel?

MOM: Well, it was just a mistake. I feel bad for her, though. She wrote this whole big report about the wrong book, and it was good, too.

ME: Do you love her any less?

MOM: Of course not. I would never love my daughter less because of a mistake.

ME: When you heard about her mistake, what was the first thing you said?

MOM: Well, I told her I could see she was upset. Then I told her about all the things she's done right—about all the assignments she's done correctly and on time. I told her that, given all the things she's done well, this book-report mistake is no big deal.

ME: That's wonderful.

The next time I met with Jamie individually, I asked her to tell me how she felt about her teachers. Based on her descriptions of each one, I was able to rank them from "least scary" to "scariest." Then I asked her how she'd feel making a small mistake in front of her "least scary" teacher.

JAMIE: Well, with Mrs. Green, it would be no big deal. I mean, she's so nice. I know she wouldn't yell.

ME: Great. So why don't you risk making a small mistake in front of Mrs. Green? Answer a question when you aren't absolutely sure you're right.

I was asking Jamie to do something she'd never done before. In case she became anxious, I said, she could think about something pleasant—something like jumping the waves in the ocean—before and after making her mistake.

Jamie said she'd try it.

The next week, I asked her what had happened. She said Mrs. Green had asked how many yards there are in a mile, and she thought about jumping the waves in the ocean and raised her hand and said, "Twelve hundred." Mrs. Green said, "Good guess, Jamie," and smiled, and then she told the class the correct answer.

ME: So how did it feel when you did that?

JAMIE: A little embarrassing, but it was no big deal.

ME: Do you think you could do it again?

JAMIE: I guess so. It's sort of like a game.

ME: Good.

Over the next few weeks, I asked Jamie to risk making a mistake in front of each of her teachers, starting with the least intimidating one, gradually working up to the ones who were most intimidating. And each week, she came back and reported that nothing terrible had happened. Eventually she felt relaxed enough to make a mistake in front of her "scariest" teacher. When she did, no one made fun of her, or punished her, or yelled.

I asked Jamie to tell her parents about one of her mistakes.

When she did, they told her it was "no big deal." "Indeed," said her father, "I once made a mistake like that," and then he launched into a story about a mistake he'd made when he was Jamie's age. "And I'm here to tell the tale," he said. "I guess it didn't matter."

Over the next few weeks, Jamie's mother told her about

- the man she almost married, before she met Jamie's father. "Boy, was that engagement a mistake."
- the embarrassment she felt when she realized she'd forgotten to leave a tip in an elegant restaurant.
- how many mistakes she'd made trying to find the right secretary. She told Jamie about all the candidates she'd interviewed, and about how hard it was to know if she was making the right choice.

Jamie's father told her about

- a "sure-fire" product he came up with that had lost his company a lot of money ("You win some; you lose some.").
- the time he got on the wrong train to come home and ended up going fifty miles in the wrong direction.
- the disaster that resulted when he tried to renovate their house—himself.

Now, whenever Jamie talked about a mistake, her parents empathized. ("It must have been upsetting when that happened.") And they reminded her of all the things that she did well. ("Well, you may feel badly about how you did in math today, but your English grade's terrific.")

Then they helped her set reasonable goals. "Jamie, don't worry about getting one hundred on that test tomorrow. It's a really hard subject. An eighty would be a very good score. If you get an eighty, we'll be happy." When Jamie came home with an eighty-two, she was excited. Not too long ago, she would have been upset. She was learning to relax about her mistakes, and to revel in her successes.

To her parents' amazement, Jamie seemed more confident and more content despite the fact that she was "messing up" more often (because she was taking risks). She was learning that she didn't have to be perfect. *She still wanted to succeed, but when she made a mistake, she didn't think of herself as a failure.*

She enjoyed school more, and though she was less "obsessed," her grades were as good as ever. She was becoming a popular choice for committee projects. She seemed relaxed, confident (but no longer overbearing), and happier than she had been in years. Her teachers were delighted.

When she brought home her next report card, her parents praised her A's and didn't criticize her B's. "As long as you're learning in class, it doesn't matter if you get a B," said Jamie's father. And then he added, "Come to think of it, I probably did get a couple of B's when I was younger." That was the first time he had admitted that to Jamie.

"I want to do better next time," Jamie said. "But these B's aren't the end of the world."

"You're right," her father said. "They aren't."

Your child is going to make mistakes. You can't do anything about that—nor would you want to (making mistakes is an important part of learning). But you can change the way he feels about those mistakes after he makes them.

The techniques in this chapter are meant for children who are hard on themselves, who are perfectionistic, who take their mistakes too seriously. If your child is already relaxed about his faults and failures, if he isn't trying to be perfect, you can skip this chapter. But if your child takes his mistakes too hard, if he lets every mistake weaken his self-image, if he has unrealistic goals and drives himself too hard—keep reading.

This chapter will show you how to teach your child that mistakes are no big deal—that she can make mistakes but still feel competent, worthwhile, optimistic.

What you may be doing wrong

Some parents set themselves up as all-knowing, all-powerful paragons of perfection. If you're one of *those,* your intentions are good. You want your child to have someone to look up to, someone to admire.

But you may not be getting the results you hoped for.

You may be intimidating your child, setting an impossible standard. In his mind, he will never fulfill your expectations of him.

Many children—particularly children of successful parents—have a hard time taking risks. Because their parents never talked about making mistakes, they think they need to do things perfectly or not at all.

By stressing your own infallibility, you may be making it hard for your child to succeed.

For your child to feel good about himself, he needs to know that he can fail, that he can make mistakes and still be loved. He needs to be able to say, "I'm not a bad person because I make mistakes. I'm simply human. *Even my parents make mistakes,* and I still love them."

Talking about mistakes

At first, you may be embarrassed to talk about your mistakes around your child. That's only natural. But it's all right for your child to discover that you aren't perfect, that you have feet of clay. In fact, it's more than all right; it's essential. You want your child to know that you trip and fall, blunder and foul up. Seeing you talk, and even laugh, about your mistakes can be incredibly helpful to your child.

Steve, nine, compares himself to his father dozens of times a day, and always finds himself lacking. At nine, he already feels like a failure.

If his father talked about some of the mistakes he makes, some of the things he isn't very good at, Steve would start to feel less like a failure.

Jackie, eleven, has an intense fear of being wrong. When her family plays games like Trivial Pursuit, she refuses to answer a question unless she's sure she knows the answer.

When her parents play Trivial Pursuit, they often guess. But they haven't told her that. If they did, Jackie might realize that it's okay to take chances.

Anthony, sixteen, is afraid of failure. So he has avoided taking difficult math and science courses, despite a lifelong interest in those subjects.

If his high-achieving parents told him about their academic failures, as well as their successes—Anthony might relax enough to be able to pursue his interests.

Janice, seven, always has to be right. If anyone disagrees with her, she argues until she wears the person out. She can't accept that she's wrong—which makes her unpopular with other children.

Her father has a sign in his office that says I'M ALWAYS RIGHT. *If he had one that said "*I'M OFTEN WRONG, BECAUSE I'M HUMAN*" Jackie might be easier to get along with.*

Jon, five, is already a sore loser on the playground. He feels he has to win every time, no matter what.

His father, a professional athlete, has a scrapbook full of clippings about the games he's won. If he also showed his son his bottom drawer—which is filled with articles about his losses—Jon might develop a more realistic attitude about competing.

Corinna, seventeen, is so intimidated by her high-achieving parents that she can't make decisions about her future. The fear of being wrong or looking foolish overwhelms her.

If her parents talked about some of the wrong turns they took on the road to success, Corinna would have an easier time planning her future.

Henry, fourteen, has a hard time finishing his homework, because he doesn't want to turn it in until every answer is right He often stays up until midnight trying to solve one or two hard problems. He is frequently tired, humorless, or upset.

If his perfectionistic parents helped him set realistic goals—80 or 90 percent right, rather than 100—Henry might learn more and feel better.

If you make your life look too easy, you may be making your child's life too hard.

Try to say things like:

- "I tried this, and it didn't work, so I tried that."
- "I wasn't very good at that, but I was better at this."
- "I made lots of mistakes before I got this right."
- "It took years before I was sure I made the right career decision."
- "So much of what I do in the office every day is trial and error."
- "Sometimes I work for months on one project, and it doesn't pay off. But then another project does."

- "I used to really hate making mistakes. But since I make them every day, I've learned to remain calm about them."
- "At the end of the day, if I've done more things right than wrong, I feel terrific."
- "Anyone who tries to do anything worthwhile makes mistakes."
- "When I was growing up, I thought my mother—your grandmother—was perfect. It took me a long time to realize that she wasn't."
- "Once I realized I couldn't handle every assignment perfectly, I relaxed and started doing better work."
- "If I was afraid to make mistakes, I wouldn't be head of my own company. I would probably still be working as a secretary."

Try to *avoid* saying things like:

- "Next time, see if you can get it right the first time."
- "Of course I'm right. I'm always right, because I'm your father."
- "Forget about how you play the game. Winning *is* everything; I don't care what anybody tells you."
- "I'm glad you got a ninety on this test, but next time, try to get one hundred."
- "When I was your age, I didn't mess up as much as you do."

Are you saying that my child should simply shrug off his mistakes?

No. He should face up to them, learn from them, and try not to make them again. But he shouldn't dwell on them. Dwelling on his mistakes will hurt his self-esteem and inhibit his learning.

If I tell my child to take his mistakes less seriously, won't he become careless about his work?

In my experience, children who are perfectionists do better when they're freed from the tyranny of having to be perfect. Perfectionism doesn't breed success, just disappointment and procrastination.

Won't accepting his mistakes actually hurt my child's self-esteem?

No. What hurts a child's self-esteem is the belief that her mistakes make her a failure. By helping her accept her mistakes as human, you will be protecting her self-image.

Won't my child respect me less if I talk about my mistakes?

No. He'll respect you more for being honest. Your child doesn't want you to be perfect, perfection is intimidating. If you share your successes and failures, your way of making decisions—imperfect as it is—your child will respect your candor.

Step One:

Talk about your mistakes, your failures, your bad decisions. If you need to, leave yourself a note on your night table, or in your wallet: "Be honest about your mistakes."

- "It took me two years to settle on the menu for the new restaurant. A lot of the dishes I tried weren't very good. There was so much trial and error."
- "The new secretary I hired isn't working out. Hiring people is one of the hardest things I've ever had to do. If I'm right fifty percent of the time, I feel terrific."
- "I loved this suit in the store, but now that I've gotten it home, I don't like it at all. I guess I'll have to take it back."

When you make a mistake in front of your child, don't hide it, fret over it, or make excuses.

Accept that you made an error, then say to yourself, "It's okay; I'm human. This isn't the end of the world."

If you have trouble talking about your imperfections, you may need to put yourself in a position where your child actually sees you making a mistake.

Play a game with your child: The object of this game isn't to get every question right; it's to show how relaxed you can be when you get one wrong.

YOU: *(To child)* Here's a new trivia game that's harder than you can imagine. Will you ask me some of the questions?
CHILD: Sure. *(Reading from card)* What year did the Boston Tea Party take place?
YOU: I don't know. But I'll take a guess—1774.
CHILD: No, it was 1773.
YOU: Well, I got it wrong, but I'm sure I'll get some other ones right. Let's keep trying.

You may want to invite your child to your office for a day. While he's there, talk about how you make decisions, and admit that you're sometimes wrong. Let him know that even smart, successful people make mistakes.

Step Two:
Encourage your child to talk about his mistakes and how they make him feel.

PARENT: If you made any mistakes today in school, you can tell me about them.
CHILD: Well, I did everything right today.

PARENT: I'm sure you were great today. But nobody's perfect. Did you do *anything* wrong?

(Child is silent)

PARENT: If you did do something wrong, it's okay. I made lots of mistakes today.

CHILD: Well, my mind was wandering and I forgot the words to the Pledge of Allegiance. And everybody saw me. I was so embarrassed.

PARENT: I'm sure that was embarrassing, but it could happen to anyone.

or

PARENT: Boy, did I make a big mistake at work today. I turned in the wrong report. Do you have any idea what that's like?

CHILD: Sure. I did the wrong set of math problems last week.

PARENT: How did that feel?

CHILD: It was so embarrassing.

PARENT: I understand how bad that must have felt, but it could happen to anyone.

Step Three:

Praise your child as often as you can (see chapter 2). If your child is accustomed to receiving positive reinforcement, he'll have an easier time talking about his failures.

Try to praise him every time you discuss a mistake:

- "Yes, you did make that mistake, but you do so many other things well."
- "I can see you're upset about your math grade, but you're doing so much better in English."
- "I know that mistake threw you. But you did lots of things right today. Why not think about those?"

Step Four:

Put your child's mistakes in context:

PARENT: I'm sure it was embarrassing when you turned in the wrong homework. But you've done so many other things well in class this term. So doing the wrong homework one night isn't the end of the world.

CHILD: No, it *was* a big deal. I felt awful when I turned in the wrong homework.

PARENT: I can understand how you felt. It must have been embarrassing.

CHILD: Yes, it was.

PARENT: But I hope you can remember that you've done so many other things well.

CHILD: Yes, I guess you're right.

Step Five:

Whenever you discuss your failures with another person, "model" the "correct" attitude for your child.

YOU: Boy, did I make a mistake. I took on too many projects, and I don't think I'll be able to finish all my work before the deadline.

YOUR SPOUSE: I'm sure you're upset. But remember how many nice things you've done for your boss this year. I'm sure he'll understand.

YOU: Yeah, you're right. I've made mistakes like this before, and I've gotten through them.

Step Six:

For a child who's *very* afraid of making mistakes:

Encourage your child to risk making mistakes—to show him that nothing terrible will happen to him if he's wrong.

PARENT: *(Playing a trivia game with son, Pete)* Okay, it's your turn. What's the capital of Florida?

PETE: I don't know.

PARENT: Don't you want to guess?

PETE: No. I'm going to get it wrong.

PARENT: But you might get it right. And if you are wrong, so what? No one will make fun of you.

PETE: Do you promise?

PARENT: Yes, I promise.

PETE: Okay. Miami.

PARENT: No, it's Tallahassee. But it's no big deal. We're all getting lots of questions wrong. In fact, you're still in the lead.

PETE: You're right. There was no harm in guessing.

PARENT: I'm really glad you see that. If you don't guess, you might be cheating yourself out of points.

PARENT: *(Helping daughter, Miranda, study for the SAT)* On this kind of standardized test, you should guess if you aren't sure of the answer. Because you have a one-in-five chance of getting each question right by guessing. And if you're wrong, you don't lose credit.

MIRANDA: I know. My guidance counselor said the same thing. But I just hate to guess. I don't want to put an answer down unless I'm sure it's right.

PARENT: I can understand how you feel. No one likes to get a question wrong. But if you guess, you might pick up some extra points.

MIRANDA: I know you're right. The next time, I'll leave a couple of minutes at the end for the questions I'm not absolutely sure of. I'll guess on those, and we'll see if it helps my score.

PARENT: Terrific. I bet it will.

(Two weeks later)

MIRANDA: I guessed when I didn't know the right answer, and this is the best score I've ever gotten.

PARENT: I'm really glad. I'm sure you also got a few wrong answers because you guessed, but that's no big deal.

MIRANDA: You're right. That didn't matter at all, did it?

Step Seven:

Help your child set reasonable goals, so his "failures" seem more like successes. That way, your child will learn that even when he thinks he's done something wrong, he's done something else right.

YOU: Instead of trying to get one hundred on the test, why don't you try for an eighty? An eighty's a terrific grade.

CHILD: Okay. I'll just try for an eighty.

(The next day)

CHILD: I got an eighty-six. That's fourteen points off.

YOU: Yes, but remember, your goal was to get an eighty. So you exceeded your goal. That's terrific.

CHILD: You're right.

The existence of a perfect score is a constant reminder to your child that he isn't perfect. Whenever possible, talk about goals your child can achieve with some effort (seventy, eighty, or ninety), rather than ones he can't. Your child will still try for one hundred. But a less-than-perfect test score will no longer be a major disappointment.

SUMMARY

"It's okay to make mistakes. It's only human." If your child can accept that statement, he'll be able to make mistakes without allowing them to damage his self-image.

1. Talk about your mistakes. Acknowledge them, then deal with them as noncatastrophic. Say things like, "This could happen to anyone." or "I'm sorry I messed up, but it isn't the end of the world."

2. Encourage your child to talk about his mistakes as gently and rationally as you talked about yours.

3. Praise your child as often as you can, as a way of putting her mistakes in context. "Sure, you did make a mistake, but you've done so many other things so well."

4. When you talk to other people about your mistakes, "model" the appropriate behavior ("Yeah, I made a mistake, but I'm only human.").

5. Encourage your child to take risks, to make small mistakes (like answering trivia questions incorrectly) so he can see that not every mistake is tragic.

6. Help your child set reasonable goals, so his "failures" feel more like successes.

THE ROUND TABLE

ELLEN'S STORY

At fourteen, Ellen was having trouble at home, trouble with friends, and trouble in school.

- She was sullen and uncommunicative with her parents.
- She was gradually losing touch with her old friends, and she wasn't making any new ones.
- She was getting B's and C's, though she was capable of getting A's.

Ellen's parents tried to talk to her about her problems, but they rarely got past the accusatory stage:

"Ellen, you're losing all your friends. And your grades are horrible. What's happening to you?"

By the time her parents finished grilling her, Ellen was feeling so defensive that she either started crying or simply clammed up.

After months of trying to get Ellen to talk, her parents called me. They told me they had a lovely, intelligent daughter who seemed terribly unhappy. In their view, Ellen lacked the self-confidence she needed to make new friends, achieve in school, or even speak frankly about her problems. In fact, Ellen was so uncommunicative that they were afraid of losing contact with her as she moved into adolescence.

During my first meeting with Ellen's parents, they told me about their attempts at communication, the unproductiveness of which distressed them. After all, if they couldn't talk to Ellen, how could they begin to *solve* her problems?

I praised Ellen's parents for trying to help their daughter, and I suggested that we initiate weekly family round-table discussions—organized "meetings" with just enough rules to ensure that everyone would get a chance to talk about his feelings.

I told Ellen's parents that I would work to open lines of communication. Then I would gradually reduce my role in the the discussions. The goal, I said, was for the family to continue meeting once a week (or more) at home, without me. The family members (the two of them and Ellen) would take turns moderating the discussions.

The next day Ellen's parents told her that they wanted the family to learn to communicate better, and that they had found a therapist to help them do that. Since I had already spoken at length with Ellen's parents, I arranged to spend several hours with Ellen alone, talking about her feelings. During our meetings, Ellen told me about the difficulties she was having communicating with her parents.

From then on, I told Ellen and her parents, we would get

together once a week to talk—to create a family round table. At the first meeting, I listed several rules that I thought would help get the discussion off to a good start:

1. Feel free to speak. Anytime. About any subject (if it's important to you, it's important to your family).
2. Don't interrupt anyone, ever.
3. Don't dump on each other. That means you can't say, "You're stupid" or "You never think about anyone but yourself" or anything like that.
4. Make "I" statements. "I am uncomfortable with the way your room looks" instead of "You're a slob." Instead of criticizing others, talk about *your* feelings. (Starting sentences with the word "I" is the simplest way to do that.)
5. Don't shout. It's hard for anyone to really hear you when you're shouting.

I didn't expect the family to remember all the rules at once. As moderator, I said, I would remind them of the rules when needed—and possibly introduce a few more as we went along.

Then I seated the family around a large round table, which I knew would facilitate direct communication.

Week One

I asked Ellen if she had anything she wanted to say. She shook her head without looking up.

I asked her mother if she had anything to say. Her mother said yes, and she began talking about the stress she was under because of the family's impending move from Boston to New York.

Within minutes, Ellen's parents were embroiled in a disagreement. Ellen's father, a doctor, planned to keep his old practice going for at least six months after the move—which meant he'd be away from home three nights a week. Ellen's mother didn't like that arrangement. The decibel level in the room rose as they explained their points of view. Ellen said nothing but looked hurt.

When the argument subsided, I intervened.

ME: Let's try something. If you want to, think of it as a game. I'd like each of you to compliment the other family members. Who wants to go first?

(Silence)

ME: Kate, why don't you try.

MOM: Okay, let me think for a minute. Okay. Dave, I want to compliment you for being so loyal to your patients. You really care a lot about your practice; I can tell from the way you're handling this move.

ME: Great. You found a positive in something that's been bothering you.

MOM: And Ellen, I want to tell you how happy I am that you came here today, and how courageous you were to do it.

ME: Good. Okay, Dave, it's your turn.

DAD: *(Looking at me)* Well, for Ellen, I agree with what my wife just said.

ME: Good, but can you tell her that directly? One of the rules of the round table is to try to communicate directly, instead of speaking to one person through another.

DAD: *(Looking at Ellen)* Well, Ellen, I agree with what your mother just said. I think it was courageous of you to come here, and I'm really glad you did.

ME: Great. How about complimenting your wife?

DAD: I think you're the best wife I've ever had. *(Pause)* No, I'm just kidding. *(Pause)* I think you're a wonderful mother and you've done a great job raising Ellen. I know I haven't been home as much as some husbands.

ME: Terrific. Now, Ellen, do you have any compliments for your parents?

(Silence)

ME: Take a minute, and see if you can think of anything. *(Pause)* Do you have anything you want to say?

(Silence)

ME: How about saying, "I think it's really great that you care so much about family communication. If you weren't loving parents, you wouldn't have bothered coming here." How does that sound?

(Ellen nods)

ME: Why don't you try it.

ELLEN: Okay, I appreciate your coming here. It's obvious you care a lot about our family.

ME: Great.

Week Two

I asked Ellen if she had anything to say. She said no, so I asked her if it would be okay if I tried to speak for her. I told her I would base my statements on the things she'd told me at our private sessions. (I had cleared with her what I could disclose to her parents about her feelings.) Ellen said okay but still didn't look up. I asked her to help me by nodding when she felt I was expressing her feelings correctly.

ME: Okay, I'm going to try to speak for Ellen. Look, Mom and Dad, you're overwhelming me with your arguing. It makes me upset, and I can't get a word in edgewise.

I turned to Ellen, and I waited. After a few seconds, she nodded.
   Here's how the conversation continued:

MOM: Well, sometimes we have things to talk about. But we try to do it when you're sleeping.

ME (as Ellen): Well, sometimes I'm not sleeping, and I hear you.

(Ellen nods)

MOM: Why should it bother you if we argue a little? All parents do.

ME: Ellen, do you want to answer?

(Ellen shakes her head)

ME: I'll try to speak for you again. I remember something you told me the first time we met. *(Turning to her parents)* Mom and Dad, it's scary when you fight, because it makes me worried that you're going to get divorced. A lot of my friends' parents have gotten divorced, and I don't want that to happen to me.

(Ellen nods)

DAD: There's no reason to think we're going to get divorced. I just need to divide my time between two offices for a while, so I'll be away from home a few nights a week.

MOM: You could just give up your practice here and move with us.

DAD: I've explained this a thousand times. I can't just pick up and leave. I have a practice here that needs me. Can't you understand that?

When the arguing died down, I asked Ellen's father if he could reiterate the last thing I had said (as Ellen).

ME: Another one of the round-table rules is that the moderator can ask you to repeat what someone else has said, in order to make sure you're really listening to each other.

Ellen's dad thought for a minute, then he tried to reiterate.

DAD: She doesn't like us to fight.

ME: That's not all she said. Try again.

DAD: Well, she said it makes her upset when we fight.

MOM: *(To Ellen)* Is that what you said?

ELLEN: Yes, that's pretty much it.

ME: Is it less upsetting when they lower their voices and speak calmly?

ELLEN: Yes.

ME: *(To Ellen's parents)* I'll be Ellen again. Is it possible to shout less, Mom and Dad?

MOM: Yes.

DAD: Definitely.

(A few minutes later)

ME: I think it would be good to talk about something positive. Can each of you tell us something you did today that you felt good about?

(Pause)

DAD: Well, I was asked to be the keynote speaker at a medical conference next January, which is a really big honor. I'm excited about that.

MOM: That's terrific, honey. Let me think. Well, I spent an hour helping Mrs. Stern next door do her shopping today, and that felt wonderful. It's always nice to help out someone who needs you. Ellen, do you have something you want to tell us about?

(Silence)

DAD: We'd really love to hear something that made you feel good.

ELLEN: *(After a long pause)* I got an A on my bio test today.

DAD: An A? That's wonderful.

MOM: *(To me)* You know, I just realized something. I'm so glad we just asked Ellen to tell us something she felt good about. If we hadn't, we probably would never have known about that A.

Week Three

I asked Ellen if she had anything to say. She shook her head. So I asked her if she wanted to tell me about anything that had happened during the week. She told me that she didn't want to talk. Then her mother started speaking:

MOM: Don't you want to say anything about flunking your math test? Remember, we had a big fight about that yesterday.
ELLEN: Well, a lot of people flunk tests. What's the big deal?
MOM: I never flunked tests when I was in school.
DAD: We love you, but face it, you're just not very good at math.
ME: You were dumping on Ellen, and we have a rule against that. It's better if you talk about your feelings. How do you feel when Ellen flunks a test?
DAD: I feel sad because it makes me think I could have done more to help her.
ME: Anything else?
DAD: Well, it's upsetting, because I know Ellen can do better.
ME: Ellen, could you try to repeat what your father said about your flunking tests.
ELLEN: He said he never flunked tests when he was in school. He's always saying that. Big deal. I'm not him.
ME: Is that all he said?
(Ellen is silent, looking down at the floor)
ME: Ellen, please try. I think your father said some other things about your schoolwork.
ELLEN: He said he gets upset when I flunk.
ME: Did he say why?
ELLEN: Yeah, because he doesn't want his friends to know he has a dumb daughter.
DAD: I didn't say that at all.
ME: Remember, the idea is to reiterate, which means to repeat accurately. Can you try it again without changing your father's meaning?
ELLEN: Okay, you said you're upset, because you think maybe you could have done more to help me.

ME: Is that pretty much what you said?

DAD: Yes.

ELLEN: Big deal. All he ever notices is the bad things I do. He never notices anything good.

DAD: That isn't true.

ME: Ellen, do you know how your father described you to me the first time I spoke to him on the phone?

ELLEN: No.

ME: He said you were fourteen, and that you were beautiful and intelligent, and I think he also used the word *charming*.

ELLEN: I don't believe it.

ME: It's true. Your father thinks a lot of nice things about you, and he even says them to other people. The trouble is, he has a hard time saying them to you. That's a communication problem, and it's something we can change.

Week Four

ME: Does anyone have anything they want to say?

MOM: Well, we fought a lot less this week. We tried to control our arguing because we know it upsets Ellen.

ME: Ellen, did you realize they were fighting less?

ELLEN: Yeah, they did fight a lot less, and I appreciate that.

ME: Can you tell them that, directly.

ELLEN: *(To her parents)* You did fight a lot less. But I'm still worried about moving.

DAD: Why can't we talk about something important for a change? Like why you're losing all your friends. People call you and you don't call them back. I feel like I'm your secretary. Jeannie called the other day, and she said it was the third time she was calling. She asked if you were sick. What kind of friend are you becoming?

ME: *(To Ellen's father)* Can you ask her that in a less judgmental way? Try something like, "Don't you think your friends feel bad when you stop calling them?"

DAD: Okay, I'm sorry. I just want to know what's going on with you and your friends. Don't you think they miss you?

(Ellen looks down)

ME: Do you want to respond?

(Ellen shakes her head)

DAD: How can you not like Jeannie? She was your best friend. Why are you doing this to her?

MOM: Wait. She didn't say she didn't like Jeannie. She just doesn't have anything to say right now, isn't that right?

(Ellen nods)

ME: *(To Ellen's father)* Your questions sound very harsh. I think you really just want to know what's going on in your daughter's life, which is understandable.

DAD: You're right. I want to know so I can help her.

ME: That's great. But If Ellen doesn't want to talk about Jeannie, that's her right. Another one of the round-table rules is that anyone can declare a subject "off limits" if it makes her too uncomfortable.

(A few minutes later)

ME: Ellen, I don't want to talk about Jeannie, because that makes you uncomfortable. But can we talk about your other friends? How do you feel about them right now?

ELLEN: I just don't care about them right now.

MOM: That's crazy. How can you not care about your friends?

ME: *(To Ellen's mother)* Can you make your question sound less like an accusation? Try something like, "Ellen, how do you feel about your friends right now?"

MOM: Okay. Ellen, what's making you feel the way you do about your friends?

ELLEN: Well, why should I care about them? We're going to be moving to New York, and then when will I get to see my friends? Probably never!

MOM: Oh, I think I understand now. You're saying that you have a hard time caring about your friends, because we're going to be moving.

ME: Great. You reiterated that perfectly.

DAD: Good. I'm finally starting to understand.

MOM: But Ellen, there's so much we can do to help you maintain your friendships.

ME: Before you try to solve the problem, you should empathize with your daughter.

MOM: All right. Ellen, I'm starting to understand how you feel, and I can see now that the move might be upsetting for you. I feel a lot better when I understand what you've been going through.

ME: That was really good.

MOM: Ellen, after we move, you can come back here on weekends if you want. Your dad will be driving back and forth anyway. And you can arrange to spend your school vacations with your friends here.

ELLEN: *(Looking scared but hopeful)* I can?

MOM: Sure. Remember when Dorothy moved away two years ago? Well, you've gotten to see her since then, haven't you? She's been back at least three or four times.

ELLEN: That's true.

MOM: And what does Dorothy say about her new home?

ELLEN: She says she misses me. It's terrible.

MOM: Well, you do miss people when you move away. What else does she say?

ELLEN: She says she's made some new friends, and it's been a good experience for her.

ME: Great. I feel like you're really listening to each other. Nobody shouted this week, and no one dominated the conversation. Ellen, you're starting to feel confident enough to say what's on your mind, which is terrific. And it seems like your parents are really listening.

DAD: We're trying.

ME: I'd like you to try something else now. It's time for you to have your first round-table discussion without me. Let's talk about a time and a place where you can do that. I think you should try to keep it going for fifteen or twenty minutes, more if you can. And remember, at home, you have to make a special effort to avoid interruptions. Turn off the TV and don't answer the phone.

DAD: Well, the best time for me is after dinner, around eight o'clock. We can use my study.

ME: How does everyone feel about that?

(Ellen looks down)

ME: Do you have any feelings about eight o'clock?

ELLEN: That's fine.

ME: How about your father's study?

ELLEN: (After a long pause) Well, that room kind of overwhelms me. I feel like I'm being punished every time I go in there.

ME: What would be a better place?

MOM: How about the kitchen table? That's a family gathering place anyway, and it belongs to all of us.

ME: Does anyone have a problem with that?

ELLEN AND DAD: No.

ME: Okay. So next Monday, at eight o'clock, at the kitchen table. Who's going to be the moderator?

MOM: What exactly does the moderator do?

ME: The moderator enforces the rules, like no interrupting, and may guide the conversation a little, the way I've been doing. For example, you can ask Dave to reiterate what Ellen has said, if you don't think he heard it.

MOM: I'll do it if that's okay.
ME: Any problems?
(Silence)
ME: Fine.

Week Five

ME: How did your round table go?
MOM: It seemed fine. We talked a lot about the move and how we felt about it, and it lasted almost half an hour.
ME: Good. Does anyone remember anything they said?
MOM: Well, I said I was still worried about being away from Dave two or three nights a week for the first few months. I'm not really used to being alone like that.
ME: I wonder how Ellen feels about that. Ellen?
ELLEN: Well, it's kind of scary. I know I'm fourteen . . .
DAD: You are almost fifteen. You're not a kid anymore.
ME: Try not to interrupt. Remember, that was one of the rules.
DAD: You're right. I'm sorry.
ELLEN: . . . but I really don't like it when my dad is far away.
DAD: Ellen, I didn't know you felt that way.
ELLEN: *(Dripping with sarcasm)* Well, did it ever occur to you to ask me?
ME: Ellen, your sarcasm is only going to make your father angry. What are you really trying to ask?
ELLEN: *(To her parents)* If you wanted to know how I felt about the move, why didn't you ask me?
MOM: I guess we should have. I can't believe we got through that entire discussion, and we never once asked you how you feel when Daddy is away. Sometimes it's hard to think of the right questions to ask. I'm really sorry, Honey.
DAD: I am, too. We'll try to ask about your feelings more. It's important for me to know what's on your mind. I should have

realized it would be scary for you to move to New York and have me gone so much.

ME: That's great. You reiterated what Ellen said without even knowing it. You're paying more and more attention to her feelings.

DAD: I have to admit it feels great to find out how people really feel, without all the shouting and arguing. It's like a cloud has lifted.

ME: Terrific. It does sound, though, like you could have done more to find out about Ellen's feelings during your round table last week. I want you to keep working on that. Did anything else come up?

MOM: Well, Dave said maybe he can give up his practice here in three months, instead of six. He said that we might have to get by on a little less money for the first few months, but Ellen and I agreed to do that.

DAD: I thought the money was the most important thing. But it's pretty obvious to me now that Ellen and Kate are more interested in having me around.

ME: Good. I'd like you to try another round table this week. See if you can keep it going for more than half an hour. Ellen, I'd like you to be the moderator. How do you feel about that?

ELLEN: Me, really? I guess I can do it.

ME: Great. Remember, if you can't think of anything to talk about, take turns complimenting each other. Or go around and talk about something you did that you feel good about.

Week Six

ME: Ellen, how did the round table go this week?

ELLEN: Well, it was pretty good. We talked for almost forty-five minutes. Nobody shouted, and we all took turns. And I learned a lot more about how everyone feels.

ME: Good. Do you remember anything specific?

ELLEN: Yeah, well, Daddy said that, as the breadwinner, he felt he had to keep both practices going, even if that meant traveling back and forth all the time. He said he was raised to provide for a family, and that he didn't want us to have to make financial sacrifices.

ME: Dave, is that pretty accurate?

DAD: That's just about perfect. It's great that Ellen remembered so much.

ME: Ellen, how did you respond?

ELLEN: Well, Mom and I said that we value Dad for a lot more than his paycheck, and that we really want to have him around as much as possible.

ME: Kate, is that what you said?

MOM: Yes, exactly.

ME: Dave, how did that make you feel?

DAD: It made me feel wanted. And I realized that Kate and Ellen weren't just putting demands on me. I realized they're willing to help me work out the problem.

ME: What else happened?

ELLEN: Well, Mom and Dad said I could go to New York next weekend and stay with my aunt and uncle. They're going to take me around, and show me where my school will be, and introduce me to some of the kids in the neighborhood.

ME: How does that make you feel?

ELLEN: Well, I'm sure I'll be a lot less nervous about the move after I see New York. I spoke to my aunt and uncle on the phone, and they told me New York's a great place to live, and I'm getting pretty excited.

MOM: But Ellen also said she's not going to give up on her friends here.

ELLEN: That's true. We talked about that, and I said I wouldn't.

DAD: Well, what about Jeannie then?

ME: Ellen, I remember how uncomfortable talking about Jeannie made you. Do you think you can handle it this time?

ELLEN: I think so. I don't feel like everyone's attacking me this time, so I'm not so scared to talk about it.

MOM: Great. We've been trying hard to do better.

ELLEN: Well, I said I don't mind talking about it, and I don't. But I'm not sure there's anything I can say to Jeannie now. I mean, I haven't been a good friend to her in months. I just think it's too late.

MOM: Ellen, I can understand that you feel hopeless about your friendship with Jeannie, and I know what that's like.

ELLEN: You do?

MOM: Of course. There've been times in my life where I haven't been a good friend to someone for a pretty long time, and I've felt awful about it. Eventually I've screwed up my courage and called the person, and you know what happens? The person usually says, "I'm so glad you called," and we've gone right back to being friends. I'm not saying it's a good idea to ignore someone for months. But if it happens, you can save the situation. I'm pretty sure Jeannie will be thrilled to hear from you.

ELLEN: Well, she might be, but I don't have the nerve to call her.

DAD: How about if we called her for you?

ELLEN: (*Rolling her eyes*) Daddy, I'm fourteen years old. That's a terrible idea. I would die of embarrassment.

ME: Ellen, how would you feel if your mother helped you decide what you might say to Jeannie?

ELLEN: Okay, I guess.

ME: (*To Ellen's mother*) Okay, why don't you play Ellen, and Ellen, you play Jeannie.

ELLEN: Okay.

ME: (*To Ellen's mother*) Remember, you're Ellen. Pretend you're calling Jeannie.

MOM: Hello, Jeannie.

ME: *(To Ellen)* Now you respond. Remember, you're Jeannie.

ELLEN: Hello.

MOM: Hi, Jeannie. It's me, Ellen.

ELLEN: *(Angrily)* What do you want?

MOM: Well, I really care about you, and I want to be your friend again.

ELLEN: Well, I'm busy. Besides, we don't have anything to say to each other anymore.

MOM: Jeannie, I hope that isn't true. I really care about you a lot. I don't have any other friends as good as you.

ELLEN: Well, you have a funny way of showing it.

MOM: I know. And I'm really, really sorry. I've been so upset about moving that I haven't been myself. I've been scared and angry and upset.

ELLEN: Well, I can understand that, I guess.

MOM: Jeannie, remember when you moved here in the third grade? Was the move really hard for you?

ELLEN: Yeah, it was. I didn't know how to be friends with anyone for months.

MOM: Well, that's what I've been going through. I'm really glad you can understand.

ELLEN: Yeah, I do, I guess.

MOM: Because I really want to be your friend again. Is that okay?

ELLEN: Yeah, sure. I understand.

MOM: Do you want to come over for dinner tonight? Around six o'clock?

ELLEN: Sure. I'd love to. I'll just tell my mom. I'll see you then.

MOM: Great.

ELLEN: Wow, Mom, you did a really great job playing my part. I mean I felt so much like I wanted to be your friend again.

ME: That was excellent. *(To Ellen)* Now do you think you can call Jeannie and play your part the way your Mom did?

ELLEN: Well, I don't know.

ME: How would it be if you went over it again at your next round table? You know, the one you're going to have at home in a couple of days?

ELLEN: Okay. We'll practice it again, and then I'll call Jeannie.

MOM: Okay. And Dave, since we're taking turns, how about being the moderator next time?

DAD: Sure. But, frankly, everyone's doing such a great job communicating that I don't even think we need a moderator.

ME: You are doing a great job, but you still need a moderator. But the moderator will be able to do less and less each week. Soon you won't need to be reminded of the rules.

DAD: Okay.

ME: Try to have at least one round table a week from now on. I suggest you put a calendar on the refrigerator door, and make an "appointment" to meet each week. Of course, if you need more meetings, you can add them.

MOM: Is everyone willing to do that?

(Dad and Ellen nod)

Ellen's mother called me from New York two months later. She told me the family had been meeting about twice a week, and "We never run out of things to talk about." Ellen was starting to adjust to her new school. The main thing, she said, was that when Ellen had a problem, they were able to talk about it constructively. Sometimes she and her husband were able to suggest solutions or even help Ellen "rehearse" the desired behavior.

Not surprisingly, Ellen's mother told me that her marriage had improved as a result of the round table. As she put it, "We didn't realize how little we communicated before. But now, looking back, we realize that we hardly ever listened to each other—I mean, *really* listened. Our communication is so much better now. And we're building each other up, instead of tearing each other down."

▼▲

The way you communicate with your child can have a direct impact on his self-image.

If
- you don't give your child an opportunity to express his feelings
- you respond to your child angrily or judgmentally
- you don't give your child a chance to speak before you interrupt
- you never sit down and just listen to your child
- you give advice, when empathy is called for

you may be hurting your child's self-image.

But if
- you allow your child to express his feelings
- you respond to your child calmly and lovingly
- you give your child a chance to speak—without interrupting
- you spend a few minutes a day just listening to your child
- you give empathy at least as often as you give advice

you are strengthening your child's feelings of self-worth.

To give your child a strong self-image, you need to show him that his ideas, his feelings, are important. The way to do that is to communicate more patiently, more empathetically, more often.

But communicating isn't easy.

You may not have the time. If your family is like most, it is pulled apart in hundreds of directions. Sometimes it feels like you won't have one minute together in the next three weeks.

You don't know how. In most families, communication is random, chaotic, and (not surprisingly) ineffective. But that may be the only kind of family communication you've seen. You have never been taught to do it any other way.

But there's another kind of communication—a kind that can have a tangible and lasting impact on the self-esteem of every member of your family.

I call it the round table.

The round table doesn't have to be round or even a table. It might be a Saturday morning gathering in the living room, or a half hour out on the back lawn one evening a week. But the round table does need to be a regular ritual to succeed in the face of all the distractions in your lives. The dinner table is a natural, if you can arrange one night a week when you can all sit down together. With a little luck, planning, and a light touch, it can be one time everybody in the family looks forward to. (Kids who started out saying, "Oh, Ma, do I have to?" have been known to switch to "This is really great!" in a matter of weeks.)

The round table can be a forum for such "hot" topics as sex or dating (with an older child), a place for parents to communicate their values, even a family court to dispense justice. It can be a time to share what you've learned, and a chance for your child to articulate what he feels, to take his place as an important member of the family—and to get the kind of feedback that is crucial to a good self-image.

The round table is a place where everybody can be heard without the distractions of the telephone and the TV. It is a

place for airing grievances, swapping compliments, and for trying out new ways of relating. And it is a place where you can
begin to introduce the techniques in this book. *If you've read this
book and thought, "These are great ideas, but when am I going to find
the time to do them?" the round table can help you.*

Once it gets going, the round table will be both a valve for
letting off steam before small annoyances become crises, and a
laboratory for exploring ways of trusting, communicating, and
supporting.

What's more, its value will expand as your child grows. If you
have the foresight to establish a round table early enough, it can
become an accepted part of family life—and it may be the one
avenue of communication that remains open with a rebellious
teen.

The round table can be weekly, biweekly, or monthly. Or it
can be called whenever one member of the family feels there's
a need for one. (You can put an announcement on the refrigerator: ROUND TABLE TONIGHT, EIGHT O'CLOCK, IN THE KITCHEN. BE
THERE.)

Getting started

First, you'll need a moderator. The moderator guides the
conversation and may occasionally enforce whatever "rules"
your family chooses. The moderator may change from session
to session, or may be "elected" to a term of a month or longer.
You may want to have a rule that states "a person must be at
least ten years old to be the moderator"—or maybe not.

Each family changes the round table to suit its own needs. But
there are a few rules that work for most families.

Why rules? Some issues are so sensitive, some subjects so
explosive, that the family may revert to familiar, ineffective styles
of communication (screaming, name-calling, and so on). With

rules, lines of communication generally stay open. Tedious arguments are averted, and all kinds of wonderful things can (and will) happen.

Round-table rules

1. Any family member may speak about any issue or problem that concerns him.
That means:
Don't say: Do we have to talk about that again?
Do say: That's really important to you, so I'm glad you brought it up.

2. No one may interrupt.
That means: If you're used to jumping in, finishing other people's sentences, or trying to solve your child's problems before he's finished talking—stop. You may want to say, "I have a habit of interrupting, and if I do it again, I'd appreciate it if you'd let me know."

3. No shouting.
That means: If someone shouts, "I'm so angry about this," ask him to try to express the same feeling in another way.

YOU: Could you say that without yelling?
CHILD: I'm sorry. I'm just trying to let you know how upset I am.
YOU: I'm glad you're telling us, but the shouting doesn't help. In fact, it makes it hard for us to really hear you.

4. No "dumping."
That means: Avoid direct criticisms or negative judgments.

"You're stupid."
"You never think about anyone but yourself."

"How can you call yourself a parent?"
"Things were a lot better before you were born. I wish I didn't have a sister."
"You have no consideration for your mother."

Dumping closes off communication.

5. Instead, make "I" statements.
That means: Instead of saying, "You're awful. You always yell at me," say, "I hate it when you yell at me. It makes me feel bad."

Instead of saying, "You're a slob," say, "I feel tired and resentful when I have to pick up your dirty socks from the floor."

Instead of saying, "Why are you always late coming home from work?" say, "I feel rejected when your schedule leaves us no time for dinner together."
Statements about "you" lead to excuses and denials; statements about "I" lead to communication.

6. Be ready to reiterate.
That means: At any time, the moderator may ask you to repeat what another family member has said.
The temptation is to *react* rather than to repeat:

FATHER: I think one hour of television is enough for one night.
MOM (moderator): Philip, can you repeat what he just said?
PHILIP: He said we won't be able to watch TV anymore. I can't live with that.
MOM: *(To father)* Could you repeat what you said?

FATHER: I said an hour of television is plenty.
MOM: Philip, can you tell me exactly what your father said?
PHILIP: He said one hour of television a night.
MOM: Terrific. You really heard him that time.

7. Right of veto.
That means: If a subject makes you uncomfortable, you can refuse to talk about it. For instance, if your child asks about the state of your marriage, and you're not ready to discuss that, say so. But give your child the same right.
If the moderator feels the subject is important, he may bring it up again, at a later date.

8. Immunity.
That means: Nothing you say at the round table can be "used against you" later.
You may want to say, "I'm willing to talk about this, but let's confine this subject to this round table. When the round table is over, that's the end of it, okay?" Since that's a lot better than not talking about the subject at all, the family will respect your wishes—and not throw your statements back in your face.

9. Don't dominate the conversation.
That means: No one person should be allowed to overshadow anyone (or everyone) else. If one person speaks too much, or too often, the moderator may begin to impose gentle limits (such as restricting "monologues" to two minutes).
If one family member has a hard time talking, ask him questions to find out what he's feeling. Or offer to speak for him:

DANIEL (oldest child): Julie, I'm going to see if I can express what I think you're feeling. Nod your head if it's right.

JULIE: Okay.

DANIEL (as Julie): Mom and Dad, I want to talk. But I'm not sure you care what I say. You seem a lot more interested in Jeremy and Brett, and sometimes I feel like you ignore me.

(*Julie nods*)

MOM: I'm glad you were able to let me know that's how you feel. We'll try to let you know how much we care about you, Julie.

Don't feel obligated to fill every silence. Short periods of quiet can give less verbal family members a chance to begin talking.

10. Communicate directly.

That means: Don't speak to one person through another.

DAD: Carol, I just can't stand it when Leslie does that. It makes me angry.

CAROL: Dad, can you try to tell Leslie that?

DAD: I'm so angry.

CAROL: I know. But tell her that.

DAD: Leslie, it makes me so angry when you do that.

CAROL: Good.

Eye contact is virtually essential to direct communication. If your child turns his chair away, it may be to avoid looking at you or other family members. Ask him to try to glance at your face for a few seconds. The next week, ask him to look you in the eye for, say, ten seconds. The week after that, try to make eye contact for twenty seconds. And so on until he can comfortably look you in the eye while talking. Encourage him with positive reinforcement.

11. Avoid all outside interruptions.

That means: Turn off the TV, and, if necessary, unplug the phone. It needs to be clear to everyone that this family time is "sacred," that Marcia's best friend, Mom's business partner, and Dad's client will *all* have to wait.

Rules don't have to be introduced all at once. (The round table is supposed to be free-flowing, not mechanical or leaden.) The moderator may want to bring up each rule as needed; some rules may not come up at all.

Here are some subjects you may want to bring up:

Chores
Hair
Messy room
Television
Telephone time
Bedtime
Homework
Grades
Allowance
Friends

For adolescents:

Dating and sex
Drinking
Drugs
Hair length or style
Style of dress
Loudness of music
Choice of friends
Money

Chores
Driving
Career plans
Parties
College applications
Telephone time
Curfew

Round-table games

You may want to play one or all of these "games"—which are designed to ease communication and reinforce self-esteem:

Positives. Have each person talk about something she did well that day. The examples can be as small as remembering to put the top back on the tube of toothpaste. Applause is encouraged.

Compliments. Ask family members to compliment each other; go around the table as quickly as you can. This "game" may have some dramatic results: Your son is forced to realize that his sister is not a total drip; your daughter has to admit that her brother is not completely disgusting. The compliments don't have to be big. But they should be genuine.

The moderator may want to begin by demonstrating the right way to give praise. Not "You're a wonderful child"—which isn't believable—but "It was great that you helped me cook dinner today"—which is.

Feelings. Each family member describes a feeling he had that day. This is great for teaching your child that what's on his mind is important to the family.

Mistakes. Each family member talks about a small mistake he made that day, then shrugs it off.

"I got lost on the way home, but here I am."
"I didn't do so great on my math homework, but Mrs. Reidy is giving me another chance, and I'm sure I'll do better today." Once again, applause is encouraged.

The Question. The moderator may ask each family member The Question—Tell me something you like about yourself—or a variant like:

- Tell me something you did well today.
- Tell me something you felt good about today.
- Tell me something you're happy about.
- Tell me something you're improving at.

Whichever family member can come up with the most answers is the "winner."

Use the round table as an opportunity to try out the techniques in this book.

Empathy

The round table is the perfect place to practice being empathetic. Indeed, empathy should be the first response whenever a family member brings up a problem, or a hurt, or a difficult feeling.

Empathy cuts through suspicion, tension, competitiveness—and encourages meaningful discussion. If saying "I understand how you feel" over and over seems to be slowing down the conversation, don't worry. In the long run, slowing down the conversation to be empathetic will improve communication.

Dealing with teasing, criticism, rejection

The round table is the perfect place for family members— parents as well as children—to talk about teasing, criticism, and rejection.

If your child talks about difficult emotions, you will probably want to:

- Praise him for telling you how he's feeling.
- Empathize ("I understand how bad that must make you feel").
- Encourage appropriate responses.
- Talk about ways you've handled similar situations.
- Rehearse desirable behaviors with your child. These behavior rehearsals can involve one or more family members:

MOTHER: Susan, if it's okay, I'd like to talk about how you feel about taking the school bus. Lately you've been asking me to drive you to school every morning.

SUSAN: I don't know how I feel.

MOTHER: Well, I know this is hard. But maybe you could tell me what happened the last time you took the bus. Take your time.

SUSAN: (After a pause) Stephen started yelling, "Ha, ha, Susan looks like an alien in that neck brace." He screamed it out in front of everyone.

FATHER: It sounds like you're really upset.

SUSAN: I am. It hurt a lot.

MOTHER: I can understand how you feel. It must have been very painful for you, especially since he said it in front of everyone.

FATHER: I'm really glad you told us about that. You were very brave to talk about it. Now we may be able to help you handle the situation.

SUSAN: Really?

FATHER: Sure. But it would also help if you would tell us how you reacted when Stephen said that.

SUSAN: That's easy. I started crying.

MOTHER: How did you feel when you were crying?

SUSAN: I felt horrible. I felt like I was being a baby, and everyone was watching me.

MOTHER: I can understand how awful that must have felt. When I was a child, I was teased, and it was horrible.

SUSAN: People teased you, too?

MOTHER: Sure. And I didn't know what to do about it. But I think I know now. If it's okay with you, I'd like to teach you something called the "emotional shrug." It's a way of saying to yourself, "This doesn't matter. Stephen said this nasty thing. I don't feel good about it. But I can live with it, and I'm not going to get upset."

SUSAN: That sounds great. But can we talk about it next week? I'm getting pretty uncomfortable, talking about this so much. I'd like to hear about your week.

MOTHER: Sure. I understand how you feel.

(A week later)

MOTHER: If it's okay, Susan, I'd like to work with you on the emotional shrug. Your father's going to tease me, and I'll show you how to react.

FATHER: *(To Mother)* Ha, ha, you look like an alien in that neck brace.

MOTHER: You're right. I had an accident, and I have to wear a neck brace. Notice I looked your father in the eye when I said that, and I sat up straight. I was assertive and nondefensive, and I didn't look upset.

FATHER: And it worked. It stopped me cold. I had nothing left to say.

MOTHER: Okay. Now can we try it on you?

SUSAN: Sure.

MOTHER: Okay. I'll be Stephen. Susan, you look like an alien in that neck brace. Ha, ha.

SUSAN: You're right. I had an accident, and I have to wear a neck brace.

MOTHER: Great. How did that feel?

SUSAN: Good. I didn't feel hurt. I felt in control of the situation.

FATHER: Terrific.

Assertiveness

Encourage everyone to make "I" statements, to start as many sentences as possible with "I think . . ." or "I feel . . ." By making "I" statements, your child will learn that his feelings are important, and that he can express even difficult, unpopular, or awkward opinions and count on the family's support. Make sure your child realizes that, no matter what anyone says, the round table will meet again next week.

Body-image

Have each person name one thing he likes about his looks. Or have him name one thing he *doesn't* like about his looks—and laugh it off.

Parents' mistakes

The round table is the perfect place to talk about your mistakes, your shortcomings, your bad decisions—to make light of them, and to come to the family for encouragement and support.

There's no end to the games, techniques, and ideas you can introduce at the round table. Once it's rolling, you'll find that it takes on a life of its own and becomes one of the most important parts of your family's routine.

The hardest part is getting started. But once you do, your family will be far better equipped to face the inevitable problems of everyday life. You may find yourselves liking, respecting, and supporting each other more than you ever imagined.

SUMMARY

Hold a family round-table discussion at least once a week. Appoint a moderator to guide the conversation and enforce rules (suggested rules appear on pages 241–246).

Use the round table as a time to share feelings, to work out problems, and to practice the techniques in this book. Many of the techniques can be introduced as games (see pages 246–247).

DR. DEBORA PHILLIPS, a behavior therapist who has worked with hundreds of children and their families, has extensive private practices in New York, Princeton, N.J., and Beverly Hills. Dr. Phillips teaches at the University of Southern California Medical School, where she is assistant clinical professor of psychiatry. She has published numerous articles in professional journals, and she is the author of two previous books, both written with Robert Judd: *How to Fall Out of Love* (1978) and *Sexual Confidence* (1980). She has two children.

FRED BERNSTEIN is the author of articles for many newspapers and magazines. This is his first book with Dr. Phillips.